FREE
30 Day
Confidence
Program

The Courage to Win

A Revolutionary Mental Toughness Formula

HOW TO MASTER YOURSELF TO MAKE MORE MONEY, FAST TRACK YOUR CAREER AND WIN IN LOVE

Lisa Lane Brown

Copyright © 2008 by Lisa Lane Brown

All rights reserved. It is illegal to copy, distribute, or create derivative works from this book in whole or in part, or to contribute to the copying, distribution, or creating of derivative works of this book.

Published by Lisa Brown & Associates, Calgary, Alberta, Canada. "Courage to Win" is a trademark owned by 1250624 Alberta Ltd. which carries on business as "Lisa Brown & Associates."

The information contained in this book is intended to be educational and not for diagnosis, prescription, or treatment of any health condition or disorder whatsoever. This information should not replace consultation with a competent health care professional. The content of the book is intended to be used as an adjunct to a rational and responsible health care program prescribed by a health care practitioner. Doing anything recommended or suggested in this book must be done at your own risk. The author and publisher are in no way liable for any misuse of the material.

The case studies contained in this book are true and based on the author's memory and best recollection of events. Dates, names, locations, and details of case study accounts have been changed or fictionalized to protect confidentiality, privacy, and for dramatic effect.

Copyright Registration:1057290

ISBN: 978-0-9809983-0-6

Printed in Canada

Cover design by Deb Tremper and Lisa Lane Brown

Edited by Laura Warner, Elaine Brown, and Quinn's Word for Word

Dedicated to You, The Reader, With Love

and...

To Laura, who lived and breathed every page of this project. There are no words.

To my sister Cara, who, in the lean years, took me to Mexico and bought me a swimsuit.

To Elaine and Gary, my very talented parents, who instilled winning in us.

Contents

1 Chapter 1 The Courage to Win

5 Chapter 2 Why People Fail

9 Chapter 3 How We Deepen Learned Helplessness

15 Chapter 4 The Formula Revealed

21 Chapter 5 The Practice of Self-Acceptance: What you resist, persists

27 Chapter 6 The Practice of Self-Acceptance: The Path to Clarity Case Studies
27 "I'm depressed."
28 "I procrastinate."
29 "I'm in despair about my weight."
31 "The passion is gone from my marriage."
33 "I'm not making enough money."
34 "My self-esteem is low."
35 "I feel unlovable."

39 Chapter 7 Cultivating the Practice of Self-Acceptance: Action Steps

49 Chapter 8 The Practice of Commitment: Honour your desires

55 Chapter 9 The Practice of Commitment: The Path to Action Case Studies
55 "My in-laws are sabotaging my relationship."
57 "I'm broke."
58 "I've put off getting a degree for a decade."

59 “My career has been stalled for four years.”
60 “What is my purpose?”
62 “I lack discipline.”

65 **Chapter 10 Cultivating the Practice of Commitment: Action Steps**

75 **Chapter 11 The Practice of Competence: The future belongs to the competent**

83 **Chapter 12 The Practice of Competence: The Path to Effectiveness Case Studies**
83 “The men I like are commitment-shy, but I don’t like the men who want me.”
88 “My staff resists tasks.”
90 “I want to be wealthy, not just comfortable.”
93 “I’m afraid of choking under pressure.”
94 “My boss won’t listen.”

97 **Chapter 13 Cultivating the Practice of Competence: Action Steps**
101 Success tools from The Courage to Win™ team

Calgary, Alberta

Dear Friend,

Welcome to The Courage to Win.™ Thank you for coming.

The first thing you'll want to do is select a personal challenge to apply the *Courage to Win* formula to. For maximum results, you must apply all three practices of the mental toughness formula to your challenge.

You can collect your FREE 30 Day Confidence Building Program using *Courage to Win* principles at http://thecouragetowin.com/confidenceprogram.html

If you want help to continue your progress, you can call the *Courage to Win* office in Calgary, Alberta, Canada at (403) 261-2726. Or, you can e-mail us at info@lisabrown.ca. There are also numerous success tools available at http://www.thecouragetowin.com

We truly want you to win, and are available to help you.

Sincerely,

Lisa Lane Brown

CHAPTER ONE

The Courage to Win

A Revolutionary Mental Toughness Formula
Make More Money, Fast Track Your Career, and Win in Love

You are about to discover a revolutionary, practical formula for dismantling fear and fulfilling your deepest desires. Now, for the first time, there is a proven mental toughness formula for conquering life's elusive challenges. Money, relationship, and career struggles all share the same root cause. At last, the antidote to painful life problems—and the formula for self-mastery and high achievement—has been discovered and is now being released. This formula explains how once struggling people have catapulted themselves from lives of quiet desperation to success. (One skyrocketed to the CEO of his organization; another won his disgruntled wife back; and yet another lost 23 pounds).

The *Courage to Win* formula has been 14 years in the making. It has been researched, developed, and tested in applied work with over 6,000 people for proven results. Two solid years were spent refining its inner workings. It was revised 23 times and presented in over 1,300 live seminars. When the dust settled, approximately $258,000 was invested in research and development to achieve this revolutionary formula.

The *Courage to Win* formula will move you to a new stage in your evolution. It offers the opportunity to realize your highest self and attain abundance. Whether you want to make more money, attract love, become fit, get a promotion, or simply conduct yourself with more confidence—the *Courage to Win* formula will help you attain your goal. Today is the dawn of a new era for you. Your courage will grow, your actions will transform, and your problems will fade. You will think life is easier, but it will be you who has changed.

Are You Winning?

There are only four challenges: relationships, career, money, and emotional self-mastery.* Which one is holding you back?

Here are typical problems people have shared with me over the years:

"I'm depressed."

"The men I like are commitment-shy, but I don't like the men who want me."

"I'm in debt."

"My self-esteem is low."

"The passion is gone from my marriage."

"I feel unlovable."

"My boss won't listen."

"I'm not making enough money."

"What is my purpose?"

"My in-laws are sabotaging my relationship."

"I'm in despair about my weight."

"I can't follow through on my goals. I procrastinate."

"My career has been stalled for 4 years."

"I've put off getting a degree for a decade."

"I lack discipline."

"My staff resists tasks."

"I want to be wealthy, not just comfortable."

"I'm afraid of choking under pressure."

In this book, we will apply the *Courage to Win* formula to every one of these problems. By the last page, you will know how real people solved these exact challenges—and how to apply the formula to your own life.

This is a book about winning. Winning is moving through problems to achieve what you want. For you, winning might mean a dramatic change: more money, finding your soul mate, getting a promotion, or losing 20 pounds. Or, winning might mean a subtler change: motivating a child, getting respect from your boss, or more passion with your spouse.

*The fifth life challenge is health, which is outside the scope of this book.

Why Winning Matters

The purpose of life is happiness. This much is clear.[1] What is not clear is the relationship between winning and happiness. How does winning—solving your problems and realizing your dreams—make you happier?

Winning makes us happier because we exist to manifest our desires. We have a natural tendency to want to better our condition in some way. We seek more joy, pleasure, and happiness in all situations. When we pursue our desires, we are moving in concert with our goal-oriented nature. When we are not working on meaningful goals, we are moving against our nature, and we become discontented without quite knowing why.

Winning also evolves us to a higher self. Your current desires represent the next stage in your evolution. What you want, right now, is moving you to the next phase in your development. To attain your desires, you must become a person worthy of them. To win in *career*, you must be a highly competent, results driven person. To win in *finances*, you must transform ideas into the physical realm of money by serving others. To win in *relationships*, you must genuinely love people with compassion, empathy, and generosity.

The opposite of winning is failure. Most human misery stems from not realizing our deepest aspirations. Every time you fail with a person or goal, you question your capability as a human being. You feel bitter, distrustful, and angry. Continued losing undermines your self-esteem.[2]

This is why winning matters. It is about becoming the kind of person who can attain your most cherished goals. Our self-esteem, including our personal confidence, depends on our ability to evolve. Above all else, on the same grim conditions, we must stay friends with ourselves.[3]

...My Story

I discovered my barriers to winning years ago as an athlete in the Canadian sport of ringette. (Ringette is a team sport similar to ice hockey played in several countries throughout the world). When I skated on the ice, a powerful and graceful side of me emerged. Unfortunately, a dark side of me also appeared. This self was insecure, egotistical, and selfish. My dark side manifested in extreme confidence swings. One week I was invincible; the next, my confidence came crashing down. I never knew why, and it hurt me all the time. My insecurity reached its zenith at the 1991 National Championships, where we lost with one second left on the clock.

It's hard to express my despair over this game in words. Losing hurt, but my deepest anguish came from the fact that I had choked in the biggest game of the year. Worse, a friend of mine scored all 5 of our goals, but I wasn't happy for her. Outwardly, I pretended to be happy: "Well done, Shauna. Way to go." Inwardly, I was eating my heart out. I wanted to be a leader, but I had no idea how to become one.

Exhausted and depressed on the plane home, I broke, letting in the fear and shame I had been suppressing for years. I was only in my mid 20's, but my fearful self had become more dominant than my confident self in virtually every area of my life. There had to be more. I soon realized I was not alone. Many people are in a similar situation. They've worked hard on themselves, gained self-awareness and wisdom, yet are still underachieving.

I embarked on a mission to find answers. I wanted to know: Is there a mental toughness formula we can use to defeat every life problem?

Over several years, I scoured self-help literature, absorbing over four hundred personal development books. I did personal counseling, cognitive therapy, Al-Anon groups, neuro-linguistic programming, energy medicine, acupuncture, telephone psychotherapy, hypnosis, and thought field therapy. I practiced sports psychology, meditation, yoga, positive thinking, and visualization. I studied food sensitivities, allergies and nutrition practices to learn the effect of food on emotions. I kept journals, set goals, listened to audio programs in my car, and attended self-improvement seminars. I got a job with a management consulting firm and studied under leadership coaches. I took certification training from four leading transformation gurus. For over a year, I apprenticed under one of America's top business consultants. I learned many valuable techniques and lessons, but the self-mastery I sought remained elusive. There wasn't a mental toughness formula out there that could be successfully applied to every life problem.

I did have one thing going for me: the athlete's perspective. In sport, there is always another game, another competition, another chance. There is always hope. I channeled this perspective into the investigative journey of the *Courage to Win*. Before you learn the exact formula, it is important you understand the root cause of underachievement.

CHAPTER TWO

WHY PEOPLE FAIL

Money, relationship, and career struggles all share the same root cause. When we are not winning, it's because *we are deepening our learned helplessness over a life problem instead of reversing it.*

The Discovery of Learned Helplessness

One of the major breakthroughs in psychology in the 20th century was the discovery that most people become helpless when adversity hits. The landmark experiment that proved the phenomenon of learned helplessness was conducted by Martin Seligman and his researchers. Seligman's team began with three separate groups of eight dogs. The first group was the control group, so nothing was done with them. The second group was put in a cage one by one, and repeatedly shocked with electricity. However, the second group's cage had an escape panel. By pressing the panel with their nose, these dogs could turn the shock off.

The third group of dogs was placed in a cage and also shocked. But, their cage did not have an escape panel. No matter what they did, the third group could not turn off the shock. Next, one by one, the researchers put the dogs from all three groups in a shuttlebox, which is a box with two compartments. The first compartment's floor was lined with electric shock. The second compartment was a safe zone. The cages were separated by a very low wall that the dogs could easily jump over.

The first group of dogs, the control group (who had not been shocked at all), were placed one by one in the shuttle box and shocked. Each one quickly jumped the wall into the safe zone.

The second group of dogs (those who pushed a panel with their noses to escape the shock), were then placed one by one in the shuttle box. These dogs, because they had learned they could control the electic shock, quickly jumped the wall and escaped in a matter of seconds.

The third group of dogs—the dogs who could not escape the shock in the previous experiment—gave up. Six out of eight dogs made no attempt to escape into the safe zone. They had learned to be helpless. In fact, they became so helpless that the researchers had to physically drag the dogs back and forth across the shuttle box to show them that it was possible to escape the shock. This experiment was later replicated with people using loud noises instead of electric shock.[4]

Learned helplessness is a giving up response

Learned helplessness is the conviction that our actions do not matter. It is a giving up response. Since we have tried and failed in the past, we believe nothing we do will make a difference; we cannot win. Learned helplessness is also known as pessimism and fear.[5] Learned helplessness leads to passivity. Instead of seeking solutions to our problems, we justify our learned helplessness. For example:

Career

- You have a secure, well-paying job, but yearn for a more meaningful one. Gradually, you resign yourself to your position. Your learned helplessness: "I'll never figure out what I want," or "It's too late to make a change."
- Your assistant has missed several deadlines despite reprimands from you. You do her work, reducing your efficiency. Your learned helplessness: "She's not conscientious," or "She won't listen."
- You admire your boss, but he rarely listens to your ideas. Gradually you stop offering them. Your learned helplessness: "He doesn't respect me," or "His ego is too big to listen."

Relationships

- Your divorce was finalized two years ago, but you've avoided serious relationships since your spouse rejected you. Your learned helplessness: "I'm unlovable," or "People who love me abandon me."

- Your husband is not as enthusiastic about childcare as you are. You sign up for an evening course, but don't tell him. Your learned helplessness: "He won't help," or "He won't listen."
- Your son has been underachieving for years. You've given him advice and support, but nothing helps long term. Your learned helplessness: "He'll never change."

Money

- You want to save money, but every time you try, an unexpected expense crops up, and you start spending again. Your learned helplessness: "I'll never get ahead."
- Your investments are losing money. You want to prepare for retirement, but fear making a mistake. Your learned helplessness: "Investing is too complicated to learn."

Consider your own life for a moment. What have you quietly given up on when it comes to career, love, or money? At this point you might be tempted to think that the *Courage to Win* formula is solely about positive thinking or optimism. It is not. This book is not simply a review of helpful techniques such as positive thinking, affirmations, or the law of attraction that have already been presented by countless other authors.

Overcoming learned helplessness requires more than one technique because it is more than just "pessimistic thinking." Learned helplessness is a profound, unconscious resignation about a life problem that is extremely difficult to spot and reverse. For example, imagine someone you care about breaks a promise to you, and you are so upset you avoid the person. You do not consider that you might be infected with learned helplessness, and that there are ways to build the trust back up between you. You simply believe, "This is a person who cannot be trusted."

Why we struggle to reverse learned helplessness

There are three reasons why it is so difficult to reverse learned helplessness. First, there is real, tangible evidence to support our learned helplessness: our previous failures, disappointments, and traumas. We have tried in the past and failed; therefore, we believe with certainty that nothing we do will make a difference. Second, when learned helplessness infects us, we are beset by fear, anger, and sadness. These feelings are very powerful. If we do not manage them well, they make us passive and ineffective.

Learned helplessness is the source of negative feelings

Learned helplessness is the source of most negative feelings.* We desperately want something, but feel helpless to attain it. Consider the following definitions:

Anger	Desire contaminated by helplessness
Fear	Desire for the future contaminated by helplessness
Frustration	Lesser form of anger
Sadness	Rage at being attached to a person you feel helpless to connect to or trust
Grief	Extreme sadness
Disappointment	Milder form of grief
Abandonment	Desire to be cherished contaminated by helplessness
Rejection	Desire to be loved contaminated by helplessness
Inadequacy	Desire to feel good enough contaminated by helplessness
Guilt	Fear of disapproval
Depression	Suppressed negative feelings
Self-pity	Protest over unhappiness[6]

You now know what is happening when you feel negatively: you feel helpless to get what you want. The collective name for negative feelings is unhappiness.[7] Unhappiness is painful and distressing. This is the third reason it is difficult to overcome learned helplessness. When it strikes, we try to ignore it—and the unhappiness it causes. Instead of trying to reverse our learned helplessness, we avoid it.

---

*There are a few exceptions. We can train our mind to create negativity and misery in situations unnecessarily. Also, phobias, an unconscious anxious reaction to a stimulus such as heights, flying, snakes, etc., can create fear and anxiety in us without prior trauma. Some foods, drugs and environmental toxins can create emotional reactions in people who are sensitive to them.

CHAPTER THREE

How We Deepen Learned Helplessness

The Four Avoidance Responses

When learned helplessness strikes, virtually every person socialized in Western culture will try to avoid it—and the negative feelings that accompany it. Unfortunately, these four avoidance responses only deepen our helplessness.

Self-pity

The first way we avoid learned helplessness is to rail against it with self-pity. We are ashamed of our feelings and resent having to feel fearful, rejected, or depressed. When you are upset about your unhappiness and feel victimized by life, this phenomenon is called self-pity.

The Art of Happiness tells the story of a woman who suffered the death of her only child. Unable to accept it, she ran from person to person, seeking medicine to restore her child to life. The Buddha was said to have such a medicine. "I know of a medicine," the Buddha said. "But, in order to make it, I must have a handful of mustard seed." Relieved, the woman promised to procure it for him. But, as she was leaving, the Buddha said, "I require the mustard seed to be taken from a household where no child, spouse, parent, or servant has died."

The woman agreed and went in search of the mustard seed. At each house the people agreed to give her the seed, but when she asked them if anyone had died in that household, she could find no home where death had not visited. She was not able to find a home free of the suffering of death. Seeing she was not alone in her grief, the mother let go of her child's lifeless body and returned to the Buddha, who said with great compassion, "You thought you alone had lost a son; the law of death is that among all living creatures there is no permanence."[8] The Buddha's lesson is that loss, negativity, and unhappiness are a natural part of life. Yet, all negative feelings can be healed, provided you a) accept suffering as part of life and b) reverse your learned helplessness and solve the life problem that is troubling you.

Self-pity is a unique form of negativity. It is self-inflicted. We create it by believing that we do not deserve to feel hurt, sad, fearful, or angry. Once activated, self-pity wants more pain, and will feed off itself to create more misery within you.[9] At this point, you are blaming others and circumstance for your life problem without knowing it. You are not ready to admit that you are responsible for your helplessness and your problem. When dealing with life problems, many people never move out of the self-pity phase.

How self-pity deepens helplessness

Self-pity promotes helplessness because it keeps you focused on your feelings instead of the problem that is creating them. When you are focused on your feelings, you view your depression or anxiety as the problem, not the life challenge you feel helpless about. You say things like, "I didn't get my promotion and now I've lost my confidence," and you are more troubled by your loss of confidence than the fact that you didn't get your promotion.

Self-pity is the equivalent of emotional quicksand. It distracts you from recognizing your helplessness, reversing it, and winning. Imagine if Seligman's dogs could talk. It's the equivalent of them saying, "It's really lousy being a dog and under the control of these humans. I'm so humiliated," instead of being concerned about escaping the painful shocks.

Self-pity is the 1st avoidance response that deepens our helplessness.

Suppression

The second way we avoid learned helplessness is to suppress it. Suppression is the technical term for pushing feelings outside of our conscious awareness. In an effort to escape the fear, anger, and sadness our helplessness evokes, we suppress these helpless feelings.[10] Suppression is a popular method in Western culture for dealing with feelings. We tell ourselves to "get over" our feelings, not let others "get to us," and that fear, sadness, and anger are signs of weakness. We may even take pride in our mental discipline, believing that mental strength means never feeling unhappy. Or, we may suppress feelings by staying busy, indulging in addictions, and avoiding emotionally-charged situations.

Suppression is a far cry from our natural response to feelings, which is to experience them. If you've ever spent time with a small child, you know this instinctively. I learned this lesson years ago at my summer ringette camp for girls. We took some girls rollerblading, and one five-year-old girl, Lyndsay, could not find a pair of rented rollerblades to fit her. When it became obvious that she wouldn't be able to go, Lyndsay did what most five-year-olds do: she sobbed in disappointment. About this time, Lyndsay's mother showed up. She was tired and had another baby in her arms, and soon became impatient with Lyndsay's tears. "Stop crying," she told Lyndsay. (By this time, Lyndsay's crying had turned into hysterical sobs). Her mother then said: "If you keep this up, you won't be back tomorrow." Lyndsay sat down. After a few moments, she looked up at her mother and said, "I just want to cry a little."

Lyndsay was only five years old, but she got it. Experiencing feelings is a normal, healthy response to stress. Fear, anger, and sadness are natural when we feel helpless to get what we want or have experienced loss. However, if we are uneducated about feelings, we are tempted to suppress them instead of feel them.

How suppression deepens helplessness

At first, suppression seems to be the answer to our problems. We assume that if a negative feeling is not in our conscious awareness, it is gone. This is a grave mistake. The purpose of negative feelings is to alert you to the fact that your desires are in jeopardy. If someone you love is unresponsive to you, you feel rejected. If money is scarce, you fear for your survival. If you're struggling with a work task, you feel inadequate. Emotional pain is like physical pain: it is a sophisticated warning system telling you that something is wrong. Fear, rejection, and anger are natural when you are not winning, and they are powerful tools for navigating life.

When it comes to negative feelings, "What you resist, persists." Your unhappiness will build until you reverse your learned helplessness and deal with your life problem (or grieve the loss you have suffered). When we suppress our negative feelings, we hide our helplessness from ourselves. We are basically saying, "I am better off avoiding my helplessness, because this is a problem I cannot handle."[11] Imagine Seligman's dogs ignoring the painful shocks and lighting a cigarette instead. This would be suppression at its finest.

To win, you need clarity. You need to know exactly what you feel helpless about. If you suppress your helplessness, you are blind to it, and cannot overcome it. If you do not overcome your learned helplessness and solve your life problem, you will remain tormented by unnecessary negativity and unhappiness.

Suppression is the 2nd avoidance response that deepens helplessness.

Disowning your desires

The third way we avoid learned helplessness is to disown our desires. In a naïve bid to avoid disappointment, we pretend that winning doesn't matter. John Molo, an accomplished musician who has played at the Grammy Awards, sees this phenomenon often: "I recently flew a guy out to audition for a band. This guy was really excited to do the gig. After he didn't get it, he immediately started with, 'Well, you know, the money wasn't good anyway; it's only a part-time thing.' I really felt like stopping the guy and saying, 'You just didn't play well enough.'"[12] Here are more examples of disowning desires:

- "I want him to respect me, but I think he's too insecure. I'll just avoid him." (You disown your desire for your colleague's respect.)
- "I don't need a fancy house. Rich people are missing the meaning of life." (You disown your desire for money.)
- "He didn't call, but it's OK. He's not the man I thought he was." (You disown your desire for this person's love.)
- "Some people are just not meant to be thin." (You disown your desire for fitness and health.)

Imagine Seligman's dogs trying to convince themselves that shock-filled cages were pleasant: "A shock free cage is overrated. I'm getting used to the pain." The problem here is that we never truly relinquish our desires for love, money, or career success. The only thing you accomplish when you deny your desires is to weaken your commitment to them. Yet, nothing short of intense motivation will sustain you in your quest for success.

Disowning desires is the 3rd avoidance response that deepens helplessness.

Pride

The fourth way we avoid learned helplessness is to stubbornly pretend that we are right in how we are handling our relationships, career, and money—even when we are not winning. We protect our self-image at all cost. We don't want to admit our weaknesses, even to ourselves. We desperately want to believe we are capable of solving our own problems. Often we believe we are more successful than we actually are. It would be like each of Seligman's dogs proclaiming, "I'm the smartest dog here. And since I didn't escape the shock, there must not be any way out."

Basketball superstar Michael Jordan admits how hard it can be to overcome pride. When his coach, Phil Jackson, brought in a sports psychologist to teach the team about getting in the zone, Michael thought it was crazy: "When we first started meditating before practice, I'm closing one eye and keeping the other eye open to see what other fool is doing this beside me." Eventually, Michael dropped his pride and opened his mind: "I became more accepting because I could see everyone making an effort. I opened my mind to these teachings."[13] Michael opened his mind...we can do the same.

How pride deepens our helplessness

When we are proud, we are less likely to seek out experts, mentors, education, and advice. Without fresh ideas on how to win, we fall back into helplessness, convinced that winning is not possible. This is the inspiration for the axiom, "If you keep doing what you've always done, you'll keep getting what you've always gotten."

Pride is the 4th avoidance response that deepens helplessness.

CHAPTER FOUR

The Formula Revealed

En route to winning, we will always encounter setbacks, obstacles, challenges, and loss. It is part of the process of winning, and why we all experience learned helplessness when adversity hits. It is not whether we experience learned helplessness that matters. It is whether we *deepen vs. reverse our learned helplessness* that determines whether we will win. When top performers encounter problems, they also experience learned helplessness. But, they do not avoid it. Top performers confront and reverse learned helplessness. This is the courage to win.

The Courage to Win

A Revolutionary Mental Toughness Formula
Make More Money, Fast Track Your Career, and Win in Love

In the *Courage to Win* formula, you reverse your learned helplessness about life problems by applying the three practices of mental toughness. These practices are the following:

1. The Practice of Self-Acceptance
What you resist, persists.

The first ingredient in the *Courage to Win* formula is the practice of self-acceptance. Self-acceptance is the ability to experience your feelings just as they are, without resistance. To conquer any life problem, we must start with self-acceptance. Here is why: Every problem is confusing initially.

This is because learned helplessness presents itself the same way an illness does: with symptoms. The symptoms of learned helplessness are distressing: depression, procrastination, low self-esteem, addictions, self-limiting ideas, and unhealthy relationships. A doctor makes a diagnosis by looking for the underlying illness that is causing a patient's symptoms. We must do the same. We must diagnose the underlying learned helplessness that is causing our symptoms. Until we apply self-acceptance, we mistakenly think these symptoms are the problem. In reality, learned helplessness is the problem. We want something in money, relationships, or career, but we don't think we can get it. Our corresponding despair creates symptoms such as depression, confusing us further.

To win, you need clarity

In the beginning stage of solving a problem, our biggest obstacle is confusion. Just as you cannot cure scurvy unless you know it is caused by a lack of vitamin C, you cannot reverse your learned helplessness unless you know *exactly what you feel helpless about*. This is called clarity, and it is the first step to winning. We gain clarity through self-acceptance. There is no need to dread any negative feeling. Anger, fear, and sadness are natural when we are not winning, and they are powerful tools for navigating life. Negative feelings are requests from our soul. When we listen to our feelings, they tell us *exactly what* we feel helpless about in money, relationships, and career. Once you have clarity about your learned helplessness, you can take the right actions to solve your life problem.

2. The Practice of Commitment
Honour your desires.

The second ingredient in the *Courage to Win* formula is the practice of commitment. Commitment is honouring your desires by creating a vision and pursuing it in the world. Having applied self-acceptance to your problem, you now have clarity. You know what you feel helpless to attain—the desire your soul is asking for. But, you still must motivate yourself to *act* and pursue your desire. This is commitment, and it is the second step to winning.

To win, you must lead your life

At this stage of solving a problem, our biggest obstacle is self-alienation: disconnecting from our desires. We are still in the habit of trying to avoid disappointment by pretending we don't care about what we want. Self-alienation is expressed in statements such as, "I don't know what I want," or "I don't care." You motivate yourself by creating a vision for the problem based on your authentic desires. In the practice of commitment, you shift from diagnosing your problem to imagining a perfect outcome for it. You provide leadership for your life by asking, "What do I want?"

By envisioning a perfect outcome for the problem, you trigger an intense, burning desire to achieve your outcome. You activate the law of attraction in your favour and become a person of action. You are now committed to getting what you want rather than avoiding disappointment.

3. The Practice of Competence
The future belongs to the competent.

The final ingredient in the *Courage to Win* formula is competence. Competence is having superior technique. There are proven success principles governing money, relationships, and career. When you learn them and then internalize them, you develop superior technique. This is competence, and it is the third step to winning. At this point in applying the *Courage to Win* formula, you have a goal: a desired outcome for your problem. You are also motivated to act. However, not all actions are created equal. The future belongs to the competent.

To win, you need superior technique

Few people train themselves long enough to discover how excellent they can truly be. In the final phase of solving a problem, our biggest obstacle is pride. We don't want to admit our weaknesses, even to ourselves. We desperately want to believe we are capable of solving our own problems. If you are not winning in relationships, career, or money, someone on this earth has the solution to your problem. You must swallow your pride and find it. To win, you must take effective action. Somewhere deep inside, you realize that you can learn more about how to win in relationships, career, and money. Through mentors, coaching, reading and practice, you develop superior technique. Your newfound skill gives you confidence, which dissolves the last shreds of learned helplessness in your mind.

The *Courage to Win* formula reverses your learned helplessness in three steps:

1. The practice of self-acceptance gives you clarity. Once you diagnose the element of your relationships, career or finances you feel helpless about, you can take action on your life problem.

2. The practice of commitment motivates you to act. Clarity is wonderful, but it is not enough to motivate us. By creating a vision for your life problem based on your authentic desires, you energize yourself to act.

3. The practice of competence gives you the superior technique you need to win. Commitment is energizing, but action alone does not guarantee success. You must take effective action. By learning proven success principles in money, relationships, and career, you gain the skills you need to succeed.

What Life Challenge Are *You* Facing?

My story has a happy ending. I went on to play ringette for Team Canada for ten years, winning three World Championships. I retired from competitive sport only when age forced me to, 30 years after the day I began. I also blossomed personally and professionally. My business flourished, and my relationships, which had been a source of pain, became joyful. Most exciting, though, was the personal confidence I experienced. Just as I had success with the *Courage to Win* formula, I want this book to be practical for you. But beware: this formula is not a quick fix. To get results, you need to diligently apply the entire formula to your challenges.

Let's get started.

Select a relationship, career, or money challenge you are facing and describe the challenge as you currently perceive it in the space on the next page. Some of the examples on page two may help you select your challenge. As you read this book, please apply the *Courage to Win* formula to your personal challenge. Of course, once you hammer in a nail, you don't throw out the hammer. You can apply the *Courage to Win* formula to any future life problem you wish. Now that you've earmarked a challenge, *you are ready*. Let's get started.

Describe your challenge below:

____

____

____

____

____

____

CHAPTER FIVE

The Practice of Self-Acceptance

What you resist, persists.

Midnight, in the middle of winter, ski instructor Stu Diver had to listen, totally helpless, as his wife Sally drowned by his side. Stu and Sally were engulfed in a landslide while sleeping in their ski lodge in Thredbo, Australia. They were trapped beneath several metres of rubble and mud. Then water burst from the pipes, and Stu found himself trapped in the horror of listening to his wife's death. Silence followed. For more than two days, Stu lay immobilized alongside his dead wife in sub-zero temperatures before rescuers heard him. Freeing him took another 12 hours. Stu said, "It was Sally's will, her resilience of spirit, that gave me the strength I needed to hold on."

How did Stu heal from this trauma? By facing his sadness. In rebuilding his life, Stu returned to Thredbo—even buying a house overlooking the site. He says, "Some people might think it's strange, but I don't. Thredbo is a small place and if I'm going to live here, I have to get used to it."[14] Stu's story is the essence of self-acceptance: the ability to experience your feelings without resistance.

The root of underachievement

Earlier, I said that money, relationship, and career struggles all share the same root cause. When we are not winning, it's because we are *deepening our learned helplessness over a life problem* instead of reversing it. Learned helplessness is the conviction that our actions do not matter. Since we have tried and failed in the past, we believe nothing we do will make a difference; we cannot win. Learned helplessness is also known as pessimism and fear.[15] It is not whether we experience learned helplessness that matters. It is whether we *deepen vs. reverse our learned helplessness* that determines if we win. When top performers encounter problems, they also experience learned helplessness. But, they do not avoid it. Top performers confront and reverse learned helplessness. This is the courage to win.

The first ingredient in the *Courage to Win* formula is self-acceptance

The *Courage to Win* formula is designed to reverse your learned helplessness so you can defeat any life problem. The first ingredient in the formula is the practice of self-acceptance. To conquer any life problem, we always start with self-acceptance. Here's why: Every problem is confusing initially. This is because learned helplessness presents itself the way an illness does: with symptoms. The symptoms of learned helplessness are distressing: We feel depressed and de-motivated, but cannot pin down why. We back away from our desires and sabotage ourselves. We cultivate negative relationships. We develop addictions. We have self-limiting thoughts such as, *"I'm unlovable,"* or "*I'm not good enough.*" Confused by these symptoms, we wonder, "Why am I getting in my own way?"

A doctor makes a diagnosis by looking for the underlying illness that is causing a patient's symptoms. We must do the same. We start by understanding that learned helplessness is causing our symptoms. Here's how: Learned helplessness creates fear, anger, and sadness in us, which we tend to suppress. Our suppression of these painful feelings leads to depression, procrastination, low self-esteem, addictions, self-limiting ideas and difficult relationships.

Until we apply self-acceptance, we mistakenly think these symptoms are the problem. In reality, learned helplessness is the problem: we seek success in money, relationships, or career, but we don't think we can get it. These symptoms are just signals from our soul that we are harbouring learned helplessness. For example: You argue with your supervisor because he is rejecting an idea you presented. Until the conflict is resolved, you will probably feel de-motivated. The problem *seems* to be de-motivation, but it is really helplessness about trusting him.

To win, you need clarity

We cannot reverse our learned helplessness (and the symptoms it is creating) unless we know *exactly what we feel helpless about*. You might realize you need more empathy from a spouse, more initiative from an employee, a new career direction, or leisure time to nurture yourself. This is clarity, and it is the first step to winning. The path to clarity is through self-acceptance.

What is Self-Acceptance?

Self-acceptance is the ability to experience your feelings just as they are, without resistance.[16]

When we are self-accepting, we refuse to condemn, suppress, or judge our negative feelings. Instead, we accept them for what they are: a request for change. We drop our self-image and experience ourselves "warts and all." The mental act of self-acceptance is tantamount to removing a blindfold. We confront unpleasant feelings about life problems, whether we like them or not. Self-acceptance gives us clarity in the midst of emotional chaos. By listening to your negative feelings, you harness their wisdom. You discover what you feel helpless to attain—the request your feelings are making. Once you have clarity about your learned helplessness, you can begin to reverse it. Whether your problem is a lack of money, unfulfilling relationships, or a stalled career—the very act of dismantling your learned helplessness will reduce any depression, procrastination, low self-esteem, addictions, and self-limiting thoughts you have been suffering from. This is why self-acceptance is healing. When we listen to our feelings and act on their behalf, these feelings are heard, and naturally heal. Using self-acceptance, you can nurture yourself through your fear, anger, and sadness for any life problem. Emotionally, the worst is behind you.

The lure of suppression

The opposite of self-acceptance is suppression. Suppression is the technical term for pushing feelings like fear, rejection, inadequacy, or sadness outside of our conscious awareness. Suppression is a mental habit. When negative feelings break into our awareness, we suppress them again and again into the unconscious mind.[17] We tell ourselves to "get over" our feelings, not to let others "get to us," and that anxiety and depression are a sign of weakness. We may even take pride in our mental discipline, believing that mental toughness means never feeling unhappy.

The idea that we banish feelings and memories from the conscious to the unconscious mind was popularized by psychiatrist Sigmund Freud in the early 1900's. Using hypnosis, Freud discovered that when some patients brought previously repressed feelings into consciousness and experienced them, their physical maladies disappeared.[18] At first, suppressing negative feelings seems to be the answer to our problems. We assume that if a feeling is not in our conscious awareness, it is gone. This is a grave mistake. Suppression is a recipe for profound underachievement, not to mention depression, addictions, narcissism in relationships, and low self-esteem. When we reject our feelings, we do so at our own peril.

Why Self-Acceptance?

The most common question I get about self-acceptance is: Why should I dredge up my negative feelings over a life problem? My answer: self-acceptance is the only "cure" for negative feelings. Negative feelings will take you to the root of every problem if you listen to them. The simple act of paying attention to our feelings elevates us to a higher consciousness about our problems.

Negative feelings are a request

When you experience physical pain, you realize your pain is a request: your body is crying out, and you need to give it what it needs—fast. Emotional pain is no different. Your soul is crying out, and you need to give it what it needs. Remember, all negative feelings are a frustrated desire: you desperately want something, but feel helpless to attain it. *Anger* is desire contaminated by helplessness. *Sadness* is rage at being attached to someone you cannot connect to. *Grief* is extreme sadness.[19] This is why I call negative feelings a "request." When you figure out what your soul needs and begin feeding it, your negative feelings will subside naturally.

When it comes to negative feelings, *What you resist, persists.* When you suppress fear, sadness or anger, you are saying, "I am better off avoiding my learned helplessness, because this is a problem I cannot handle."[20] When you reject your negative feelings, your body "turns up the volume" to get your attention. Your unhappiness will build until you acknowledge what your soul is asking for and provide it.

Are you suppressed?

I'm always surprised to find that most people do not consider themselves suppressed. They either view themselves as highly emotional (in touch with their feelings) or highly rational (in control of their feelings). I want to point out that you can be a highly emotional person and still be suppressed. In fact, excessive emotionalism is usually a sign of resistance to feelings, mostly in the form of self-pity. It grieves you to feel emotional pain, and your tears are a form of protest. If you prize rationality, you secretly believe that negative feelings are self-indulgent and weak. You will expend much effort to avoid feeling vulnerable or out of control. You believe that once you are in the grip of intense feelings, you will lose your rationality and effectiveness. You do not know that there is a better way to handle fear than suppression. Most of us suppress our feelings far more than we are aware. Since suppression is an instinctive part of being human, it's a good idea to assume that we are suppressed at least some of the time.[21]

The bottom line

When we are suppressed, we stay confused about life problems. Because we do not *really* know what we feel helpless about, we remain passive, and the problem intensifies. We also spend our lives battling the symptoms of learned helplessness. Our conviction that nothing we do matters, leads to fear, sadness, anger and frustration—which we instinctively suppress. Our suppression leads to mild depression, procrastination, addictions, unhealthy relationships and low self-esteem. Instead of working to solve our life problem, we spend our days pre-occupied with these symptoms. Unless we diagnose our learned helplessness, we cannot evolve: life becomes a perpetual struggle, and winning remains elusive.

The opposite of suppression is self-acceptance. If we choose self-acceptance, we choose clarity. We are able to finally diagnose the learned helplessness that is causing our life problems. By accepting our feelings, we also heal them. The body stops sending us massive waves of negative energy in an attempt to wake us up about a problem. By approaching our feelings with compassion, we can nurture ourselves through any failure, because we are diagnosing its source and can now learn to prevent it when possible. If winning simply is not possible, we can use self-acceptance to grieve this loss and heal it over time. Much freedom comes from not having to mislead, rationalize, or deceive yourself about your reactions to life problems. When you truly open and listen to your feelings, you enjoy an inner clarity that is heavenly. You also heal the fear, anger, or sadness that has been plaguing you.

CHAPTER SIX

THE PRACTICE OF SELF-ACCEPTANCE:

THE PATH TO CLARITY

The following seven case studies show how self-acceptance creates clarity with respect to a life problem. By listening to negative feelings, these individuals discovered the core of their fear: what they felt helpless to attain. The case studies are:

"I'm depressed."
"I'm procrastinating."
"I'm in despair about my weight."
"The passion is gone from my marriage."
"I'm not making enough money."
"My self-esteem is low."
"I feel unlovable."

"I'm depressed."

Seven months ago Carolyn* moved to Texas to take care of her elderly parents. Though she welcomed the change, Carolyn was plagued by mild depression. This confused Carolyn because she had much to be grateful for: her health, family, and friends.

I explained to Carolyn that depression comes from suppressing feelings. Depression and numbness are shutting down mechanisms against fear, anger, and sadness. We cannot pick and choose which feelings we want to

---

*Names, details, and circumstances of all case study individuals in the *Courage to Win* have been changed to protect confidentiality.

suppress in life. The only way to "avoid" any negative feeling is to mute our entire feeling function. Our corresponding numbness is mild depression.[22]

I asked Carolyn to invoke self-acceptance by opening to her feelings. "What do you feel most pessimistic about these days?" I asked her. The first thing Carolyn wrote down surprised her: after only seven months, she was experiencing caregiver burnout. This was difficult for her to admit. A nurse by occupation, she took pride in supporting others. As well, her parents were supporting her financially, and she felt beholden to them. I suggested to Carolyn that she experience her feelings of impatience and annoyance more fully. What was her soul asking for?

Carolyn realized how hopeless she felt about getting even her basic needs met: "I rarely ask for time off, and when I do, my mother gets a pained look on her face. Nothing I say will make her understand my situation." Carolyn knew that unless she got what she wanted—more time to nurture herself—her depression would persist. She took immediate action: "I usually complain to my sisters about the burden of caring for our parents. Today I asked them both to relieve me over Easter. They both agreed. I'm amazed they supported me and I'm really excited about the Easter weekend!" Many people assume radical life changes are required when they are mildly depressed. I have found that starting with small requests, the way Carolyn did, empowers us to go after our larger dreams.

Core of Carolyn's depression:
Helplessness to assert her need for time off

At first, Carolyn thought her problem was mild depression. However, Carolyn's depression was a symptom created by suppression—she had been suppressing her helplessness about taking time off. By invoking self-acceptance, she quickly realized that her core problem was learned helplessness about asserting her needs with family.

"I procrastinate."

An intelligent young graduate student named Maggie attended the *Courage to Win* seminar with the goal of finishing her thesis in 32 days. She had been procrastinating on it for months. Maggie thought her problem was lack of discipline. She kept making up writing schedules that would only last a day or two. I suggested to Maggie that she experience her feelings about her thesis by imagining herself writing. After a few moments she reported feeling "uncomfortable." I said, "Bring a sharper observation. What is the exact feeling?"

She replied, "Inadequacy. My topic is too broad in scope. Based on my research, it cannot be adequately covered in one thesis. Even my supervisor agrees that it's extremely broad." Maggie opened her eyes and smiled. Using self-acceptance, she had discovered the source of her learned helplessness: her thesis topic was too broad. That day, she scheduled a meeting to ask her supervisor for a narrower topic.

Core of Maggie's procrastination:
Helplessness to narrow her thesis topic

Initially, Maggie thought her problem was lack of discipline. But by experiencing her feelings of inadequacy, Maggie pinpointed the cause of her procrastination: helplessness about covering such a broad topic. Most people try to defeat procrastination by attacking it directly. They make up lists, schedules, and deadlines. The challenge with this approach is that you are trying to change your procrastination before you have properly diagnosed its root cause. By experiencing your feelings, you can understand why you are procrastinating and overcome the real barriers to action.

"I'm in despair about my weight."

Gail didn't drink or use drugs, but she used food like a drug. She loved ice cream, chocolate, and other treats, and would look forward to them all day. I suggested to Gail that she put off eating sugar for 30 minutes each day and experience the feelings that erupted during this time. She agreed to keep a journal about these 30 minute periods. After a few weeks, Gail said that food nurtured her when she felt alone. Gail was deeply in love with her husband, Alan, but knew there was something missing in her marriage. Finally, it dawned on Gail that Alan was frequently disconnected from her. When Gail spoke, Alan was often distracted. He'd watch sports when she talked about an issue that was upsetting her, or forget to do little things around the house. Sometimes when she tried to hug or kiss him, he would seem annoyed. When Alan pursued her for closeness, Gail would relax and not need comfort foods. When he didn't, she would become anxious, eating treats throughout the day. Gail finally saw the cause of her food addiction: her helplessness to get Alan to respond to her consistently. Her feelings of aloneness were a request for more intimacy.

When I assured Gail that she could create more connectedness with Alan, her eyes welled up with tears. "Sign me up," she said. "What do I do?"* Within a year, Gail's marriage was flourishing, and her compulsive eating subsided.

Core of Gail's food addiction:
Helplessness to connect with her husband

Originally, Gail was convinced her food addiction was only about pleasure. By listening to her feelings, she uncovered her helplessness about getting Alan to respond to her. This epiphany empowered her to make changes in her marriage that brought about much happiness for her.

Most people try to approach addictions by quitting "cold turkey." Quitting is a noble cause, but most people fail because they quit their addiction before understanding the feelings driving it. They do not realize that every major addiction masks a painful life problem—and a deep learned helplessness about solving it. Addictions mask our problems by giving us the energy to suppress them. When we indulge in smoking, drugs, alcohol, over-napping, compulsive spending, extreme doses of T.V., pornography, destructive gambling or sex obsession, we gain the energy we need to function while suppressed.[23] Instead of using self-acceptance to nurture ourselves, we nurture ourselves through addictions.

Want to test this idea? Cut out coffee, soda pop, sugar, alcohol, drugs, cigarettes, shopping, naps, and TV for one week—and do not use substitutes. It may surprise you just how anxious or depressed you feel without them. Some addictions mask a physical problem. You may suffer from symptoms such as fatigue, headaches, or back pain, and your addiction helps you function despite your ill-health.

---

*For the exact strategies Gail used to create more responsiveness in Alan, see the Pursuit Dynamic in the Practice of Competence chapter. Also, addictions are not only caused by relationship stress. They are often caused by financial or work stress.

The physiological element of addictions

While we may *start* an addiction to suppress emotional or physical pain, the addiction quickly becomes physiological in nature. With repeated use, the substance becomes a necessary ingredient of the body's chemistry; when the substance is withheld, we go into withdrawal.[24] An addiction can also perpetuate itself by creating new symptoms. High doses of aspirin can create rebound headaches that make us want more aspirin. Caffeine wreaks havoc with our adrenal system, fatiguing us and creating cravings for more caffeine.

When you have an addiction and quit it "cold turkey", the symptoms can be excruciating. Not only is your body screaming for the substance, you are noticing painful feelings or physical symptoms for the first time. This discomfort can be so strong that you find yourself returning to the addiction despite your best intentions. Over time, an addiction morphs into its own separate problem by damaging our health, self-respect, and relationships. Now we have two problems: our original life problem and the damage of our addiction.

By using self-acceptance, you can discover what problem your addiction is masking for you. Simply put off using the addictive substance or behaviour and allow the feeling or physical symptom to show itself.* When it does, accept the feeling with compassion and ask, "What desire do I feel helpless to fulfill?" Next, strive to give yourself what your soul needs. Over time, if you are patient and making progress with your life challenges, you will not need the addiction to cope with stress. You will be easing your stress directly by solving life problems.

"The passion is gone from my marriage."

Chad sought help to bring his marriage back to life. He said he no longer felt any passion for his wife, and doubted it could be re-kindled. Compounding the issue was the fact that Chad had felt tremendous passion for a woman he had had an affair with years earlier.

*Some people have had excellent success with a treatment for addictive urges that is based on the body's energy system. It is called Thought Field Therapy. For details, consult the book *Stop the Nightmares of Trauma: Thought Field Therapy* by Roger J. Callahan, Professional Press, 2000. A full treatise on addiction is beyond the scope of this book, and I do not wish to oversimplify it. If you are abusing a substance daily, then a rehabilitation program will be needed to detoxify your system and remove painful withdrawal symptoms so you can focus on tackling life challenges.

Initially, Chad scoffed at working at his feelings. He just wanted me to tell him what to say to his wife to improve the marriage. I did not relent. Instead, I kept asking him to visualize a time he felt connected to his wife. After many attempts in which he felt numb, Chad began to soften.

Chad finally touched the sadness in his heart about betraying his wife. This led him to experience true empathy for her for the first time over his affair. Aloud, he wondered:

- I don't know if she will ever be able to trust me again
- I don't know if she loves me
- I don't know how she feels about our sex life
- I don't know if she stays with me for love or security

Chad finally admitted his helplessness over re-gaining his wife's trust: "I put myself in her shoes and I don't know how she could get over my betrayal. I have been so stupid to expect her to just forget about my affair." He left my office to begin the long process of earning his wife's forgiveness.

Core of Chad's numbness:
Helplessness to re-build trust with his wife

When we suppress our fear, anger and sadness about any issue in a relationship, we become numb about the other person. Remember, we cannot pick and choose which feelings we want to suppress. We can only suppress *all feeling*. In relationships, this means that when we suppress fear or sadness, we also suppress love and desire.

We think our passion or love for the other person is "gone," but it is merely suppressed, along with our fears and resentments. In Chad's case, he was suppressing his feelings of remorse, his vulnerability towards his wife, and his helplessness to re-gain her trust. This made him numb in the relationship. When his wife wanted to talk about her pain over his infidelity, he shut her out, causing her to withdraw even more. By turning towards his feelings using self-acceptance, Chad experienced his suppressed fear about the relationship. He re-gained his motivation to listen, apologize, sacrifice—whatever was needed for his wife to heal.

The moment there is hurt, fear, and conflict in any relationship, we're tempted to suppress it and simply carry on. The problem with this approach is that your feelings are a request for change in the relationship. Ignore your feelings, and you put the relationship (or at least the good feelings in it) at risk, long term. Whether you need respect, listening, trust, affection, or time, your feelings are counting on you to negotiate these things in the relationship. By accepting your feelings, you can learn what you need from friends and family, and ask for it. Your self-acceptance will keep your relationships flourishing.

"I'm not making enough money."

"It was my dream to run my own consulting business, but I'm starting to wonder if it's worth it. I drop everything for my clients; I even do work they don't pay me for. I'm not making nearly enough money to deal with this hassle," Joan complained bitterly.

It was clear that Joan was enmeshed in strong feelings. Before her problem could be solved, Joan needed clarity. What, specifically, did she feel helpless about when it came to her clients? I said, "Joan, I want you to finish this sentence five times: 'If I were 5% more accepting of my fear today, I would…" The answers came easily to Joan:

- I would give them an accurate estimate of my time when bidding on contracts
- I would stop 'low balling' my travel costs
- I would stick to the scope of work I've agreed to

Core of Joan's money struggles: Helplessness over making sales

By opening up to her feelings, Joan gained total clarity about what was missing in her business: the skill and determination to adequately sell and negotiate her services. Joan realized just how helpless she felt to ask her clients for more money—in the form of higher fees, travel costs, and less work. Joan reports: "I had a grueling meeting with the client. I was able to maintain confidence under attack and make some critical points without demeaning anyone (although at first, they didn't like me holding them accountable). Afterwards I was tired, but tremendously relieved. I had taken back control of the situation. In my mind I have drawn a line about what I need to ask for. I've finally accepted an important skill when it comes to making money: Ask and you shall receive." By opening up to her frustration about running her business, Joan pinpointed her helplessness over selling for the first time. This paved the way for her to dramatically alter the way she approached the sales process.

The core skill to making money as an employee or entrepreneur is sales. Selling is a skill, just as making a presentation, designing a building, or planning a project is a skill. The more competence you develop in sales, the more money you will make over your working lifetime. If you are experiencing burn out, survival fear, or any other feelings with respect to money, I strongly suggest you consider how your sales skill (or lack of it) is affecting you. By being brutally honest with yourself, you can transform your financial future.

"My self-esteem is low."

When I was fifteen, my parents split up. My mother moved 2,000 miles away and my father plunged into an intense affair with his new girlfriend. The first nine months after the divorce, I did not cry. In fact, I did not think about the divorce at all until my sister said, "Dad thinks you hate him." Her words shocked me. As far as I was concerned, I wasn't upset at all. I even prided myself on my stoic nature. I only broke down once, when my mother said in her most gentle voice, "Dear, why won't you call me?"

Three years later, I found myself flipping through a book on self-esteem at a bookstore. I finally realized something I had been avoiding since the divorce: "I'm not feeling good about myself." To others, my low self-esteem back then was obvious. I was skinny, yet running six miles a day trying to lose weight. I had few friends, and I wasn't dating. Even my unshakable athletic confidence had faltered.

I made an appointment for counseling, where I finally touched the loss of our family. When the tears finally came, my sadness was so great I feared my chest would split open. I had shut out my parents; I was convinced they wouldn't listen. As I re-activated my feelings and began communicating with them, my self-esteem was restored.

Core of Lisa's low self-esteem: Suppressed helplessness over getting compassion from parents

After the divorce, I thought my problem was low self-esteem. Later, when I opened to my feelings of abandonment, I saw that my core problem was learned helplessness about my parents. I did not believe I would get compassion from my Mom and Dad about my pain. My clarity about the challenge empowered me to do something about it. Gingerly, I began the process of building up the lost trust.

People often ask me, "Lisa, I'm a nice, conscientious person. Why do I have low self-esteem these days?" Low self-esteem is often the by-product of suppressing our feelings. Our mind is our basic tool for survival. When we betray the mind by suppressing our feelings, our self-esteem naturally suffers.[25] If your self-esteem is struggling, you can be sure you have withdrawn consciousness from a problem and are refusing to face your helplessness about it. The good news is that by opening to your feelings about your problem, you can instantly raise your consciousness and improve your self-esteem.

"I feel unlovable."

Sometimes we have thoughts that don't reflect our true selves such as, "I'm unlovable," or "I'm not good enough." Such self-limiting beliefs are frustrating because no amount of positive self-talk seems to influence them.

Self-limiting beliefs are created by blocked negative feelings

We cannot change self-limiting beliefs by talking ourselves out of them because they are held in place by blocked negative feelings such as rejection, fear, and inadequacy.[26] If a parent habitually treated you with anger or contempt when you were young, it's highly unlikely you had the maturity to confront your feelings of fear and rejection. Our typical reaction is to suppress the hurt of these experiences and blame ourselves. These suppressed feelings of rejection and abandonment manifest as the belief that you are unlovable, or that something is wrong with you.[27]

Most people try to shift their self-limiting beliefs using their intellect. If they recognize they are holding a belief such as, "I'm unlovable," they will try to overcome it rationally, such as repeating affirmations or writing an essay on why they are lovable. This rarely works, because you are applying an *intellectual* solution to an *emotional* problem. You cannot *think* your way to lovability or worthiness. You must feel your way out and discover what you feel helpless about in the present day.

How to heal self-limiting beliefs
Case study: "I'm unlovable."

1. Accept and experience the feelings underneath the belief

If you are holding a self-limiting belief such as "I am unlovable," you can shift it by feeling your feelings of rejection using the action steps at the end of this chapter. When you confront previously blocked feelings of rejection, you are now listening to them and what they are trying to tell you about how you navigate relationships. Only after you experience your feelings will you be able to be brutally honest with yourself...for example, are you self-centered in relationships? Narcissistic? A martr? Controlling? Clingy? If there is anything you feel helpless about in a relationship now (getting understanding, affection, acceptance or help from people), this will become obvious to you, and you can make necessary changes in the relationship. Listening to the feeling and acting on its information will help heal the belief, "I'm unlovable." Experiencing your feelings will also help you can heal feelings of loss by grieving the relationship. To break through an inner barrier, sometimes you just have to cry a little.

2. Realize your childhood trauma was not your fault

To further reverse this self-limiting belief, you must grasp on an emotional level that this childhood rejection wasn't your fault. For this, I suggest you re-train your mind. You do this by affirming to yourself daily that your parents' rejection of you was not your fault. The film *Good Will Hunting* illustrates this point beautifully. Matt Damon plays an underachieving genius who blames himself for childhood abuse. In the emotional climax of the movie, the character played by Robin Williams says to Matt, "It's not your fault." For the first time in his life, Matt's character dares to believe him.

3. Engage in healthy, loving relationships

The third step is to win in your relationships. You need to form healthy relationships with people who genuinely love you. (This is easier when you have good communication skills. The practice of competence will assist you here). This will convince you beyond a shadow of a doubt that you are lovable.

Years ago, during a ringette game, I was frustrated because I wasn't scoring goals. I was repeating positive affirmations to myself like crazy, but nothing was helping. In frustration I turned to a teammate and said, "How do you get your confidence back when you're not scoring?" She said, "I study the goalie to find out why I'm not scoring. Then I change the way I'm shooting, and shoot more. Once I score, my confidence comes back." That day was a turning point for me. It made me see how dramatically our self-image and beliefs are impacted by our results. If we perform well in business, sport, and the performing arts, we feel confident. If other people genuinely love us with compassion and generosity, we feel lovable. If we want to *feel* lovable, it helps to be *shown* love. Sometimes there is no substitute for winning.

Final Thoughts on Self-Acceptance

Self-acceptance liberates you from self-pity

As soon as you invoke self-acceptance towards a problem, you move from self-pity to accountability. This is because you have freed yourself from the need to blame others for your feelings. You can turn inward and understand what your feelings are asking for—instead of complaining that you should not have to feel fearful, rejected, or alone. I do not suggest that other people never hurt you. People transgress against us every day. I am saying that when you take the mental position that your feelings are a source of wisdom, you no longer pity yourself for having negative feelings. You are not a victim any more; you know how to harness the wisdom of your feelings and heal them.

Acceptance vs. approval

You may be wondering: "What if I despise something about myself or my life? How can I accept myself? And if accept it, am I stuck with my poverty, a bad marriage, an annoying boss or a weight problem? No. Self-acceptance does not mean you *approve of* a distressing situation in your life. You do not resign yourself to a dissatisfying relationship, career, or financial situation. You open to your painful feelings about this situation so that you may transform it.[28] Instead of resigning yourself to your situation, your newfound clarity allows you to finally begin reversing your learned helplessness about it.

The inner barrier to self-acceptance

The main inner barrier to self-acceptance is that sometimes we are not the person we would like to be. When we dislike something, we tend to resist it with denial or anger. Consider any financial, emotional, or career problem you are experiencing. Is your attitude towards it one of acceptance or resistance? Acknowledging your tendency to reject your thoughts, feelings, and results helps you cultivate self-acceptance.

The path to change

Self-acceptance is the path to clarity with all life problems. By harnessing the wisdom of your feelings using self-acceptance, you can clarify exactly what you feel helpless about. You are now empowered to act and solve your life problem. The courage to listen to your feelings always paves the way for change.

CHAPTER SEVEN

Cultivating the Practice of Self-Acceptance:

Action Steps

Here are four action steps you can use to apply self-acceptance to any problem. Please apply these steps to the personal challenge you are working on.

1. Re-train your mind and heart in self-acceptance

This exercise will re-train your mind and heart in self-acceptance with respect to any negative feeling you are having about your problem. Write 5-10 different endings to this sentence every day for two weeks, not including weekends. Do not be alarmed if you see repetition in your endings; this is a natural consequence of the exercise.

"If I were 5 percent more accepting of my fear today…."[29] At the end of two weeks, you will have brought new layers of helplessness into conscious view. Record your epiphanies.

2. Experience your feelings

The second step is to feel the feelings your problem is triggering in you. Your goal in opening to your feelings is to discover exactly what you feel helpless about with respect to your problem. It is critical that you *feel* your feelings before you analyse, talk, or write in a journal about them.

No amount of intellectual analysis will provide the insight you seek and heal you. You must open to your feelings with the abandon of a five-year-old.

This step requires courage, because you must confront the feelings and take responsibility for them. Up until now, you may have been blaming people or circumstance for your problem. The easiest way to stop blaming is to remind yourself that your feelings are a significant source of wisdom; they are designed to alert you that you feel helpless about an unmet desire. Blaming others to avoid these feelings will simply prolong the problem. There are two techniques that will help you explore your feelings: emotional visualization and opening the chakras.

Emotional Visualization

Three days per week for the next three weeks, set aside 15 minutes per day to open to your feelings using the following exercise.

Career/Work or Sport/Performing Arts

Sit in a quiet space where you will not be disturbed. Close your eyes and relax. Focus on your breathing. Breathe slowly and deeply. Once you are relaxed, go back to a memory of a performance when you felt confident, valued, powerful, and significant. Re-run this scene in your mind. Allow the feeling to grow stronger as an energetic experience. Re-access the positive energy you had at that time. Continue this for at least 10 minutes. If negative feelings surface, explore them by trying to make them stronger as an energetic experience. Try to sustain the negative feelings for at least 10-15 minutes.

Relationships

Sit in a quiet space where you will not be disturbed. Close your eyes and relax. Focus on your breathing. Breathe slowly and deeply. Once you are relaxed, go back to a time when you felt loved, appreciated, and accepted BY another person or loving, accepting and connected TOWARDS another person. Re-run this scene in your mind. Allow the feeling to grow stronger as an energetic experience. Re-access the positive energy you had at that time. Continue this for at least 10 minutes. If negative feelings surface, explore them by trying to make them stronger as an energetic experience. Try to sustain the negative feelings for at least 10-15 minutes.

Money

Sit in a quiet space where you will not be disturbed. Close your eyes and relax. Focus on your breathing. Breathe slowly and deeply. Once you are relaxed, go back to a time in your life when you felt financially powerful and abundant. Re-run this scene in your mind. Allow the feeling to grow stronger as an energetic experience. Re-access the positive energy you had at that time. Continue this for at least 10 minutes. If negative feelings surface, explore them by trying to make them stronger as an energetic experience. Try to sustain the negative feelings for at least 10-15 minutes.

Opening the Chakras

The chakras, one of the body's eight energy systems, are centers of swirling energy in the body. An imprint of every emotionally charged event in your life is recorded in your chakra energy. When you are self-accepting, your chakras are balanced and open, and you experience the positive emotions emanating from them. When energy is locked inside a chakra due to suppression, the chakra becomes out of balance, creating a surplus of negativity. People can sense your negative energies instinctively, and will react to you accordingly.[30] By working with your chakras, you can unlock suppressed energy. There are seven chakras, but I am going to focus on the first four, as they are the key ones to start with. Here are the first four chakras and their corresponding energies:

Root chakra – The root chakra is the life force chakra. Positive emotions associated with the root chakra: groundedness, primordial energy, affiliation with the human tribe, and sexual attraction. Negative emotions associated with the root chakra: survival fear, money worries, hostility, and aggression.

Womb chakra – This is the chakra of creation, innocence, healing, and imagination. Positive emotions associated with the womb chakra: joy, freedom, laughter, authenticity, creativity, faith, and trust. Negative emotions associated with the womb chakra: over-responsibility, burdened, self-pity, suspicion, and rigidity.

Solar plexus chakra – This chakra maintains the person's ego or individual identity. Who you are and want to be seen as is forged with this chakra. Positive emotions associated with the solar plexus chakra include power, significance, and adequacy. Negative emotions associated with the solar plexus chakra include anger, frustration, failure, inadequacy, and insignificance.

Heart chakra – The heart chakra is the chalice of joy and love. Positive emotions related to the heart chakra include connectedness, love, and joy. Negative emotions associated with the heart chakra are abandonment, rejection, and hate.[31]

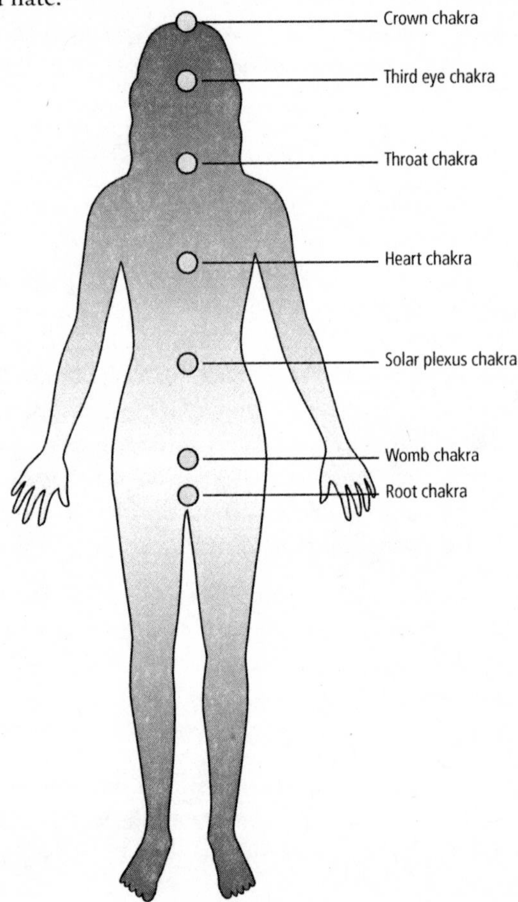

There are many exercises to get chakra energy flowing and balance them. But to begin the release of suppressed energy, very little is required. Simply place the palm of your hand on the chakra you wish to open the flow of energy within. Quiet your mind; focus on your life challenge and open it to receive any images or feelings that present themselves to you.

Repeat this exercise 5-10 minutes per day for five days. You will spontaneously experience emotions and images. If you pay attention to them, you will be able to harness the wisdom of your feelings, and insight about the nature of your learned helplessness will follow.

3. Identification: what are you *really* feeling?

Now that you have trained yourself to be more in touch with your feelings, you can identify exactly what you feel helpless about—and the request these feelings are making of you.

1. Visualize the life problem or person that is troubling you. What are the *feelings* this image evokes? In one sentence, describe the problem, including your negative feelings. For example, "I'm frustrated with a member of my team." Make sure you include a feeling word from the list below to determine what you are really feeling.

Anger	Desire contaminated by helplessness
Fear	Desire for the future contaminated by helplessness
Frustration	Lesser form of anger
Sadness	Rage at being attached to a person you feel helpless to connect to or trust
Grief	Extreme sadness
Disappointment	Milder form of grief
Resentment	Desire contaminated by helplessness related to others (others have limited your opportunities)
Abandonment	Desire to feel cherished contaminated by helplessness
Rejection	Desire to feel accepted contaminated by helplessness

Inadequacy	Desire to feel good enough contaminated by helplessness
Guilt	Desire for approval contaminated by helplessness
Compassion	Desire to alleviate suffering contaminated with helplessness
Shame	Desire to be successful contaminated by helplessness
Loss	Desire that cannot be fulfilled
Hate	Desire for revenge
Remorse	Regret over past actions
Depression	Suppressed negative feelings
Self-pity	Protest over helplessness and unhappiness[32]

In the space below, write down your problem and negative feelings: (e.g., "I'm frustrated with a team member.")

____

____

____

4. What *specifically* do you feel helpless to attain?

Most negative feelings stem from a desire contaminated by helplessness. There are a finite number of things we become helpless about. To identify yours, simply review these categories.

Money
We feel helpless to:

- Earn enough money to take care of ourselves without help
- Save money
- Create financial assets that make money for us
- Invest money wisely (become financially literate)

Career
We feel helpless to:

- Discover our purpose in life

- Sell a product or service
- Sell ourselves as employees and ascend the corporate ladder
- Motivate our colleagues, boss, or team to do what we want
- Learn new career skills

Love & Friendship
We feel helpless to:

- Attract lovers, spouses, or friends
- Inspire people to give us physical affection, time in shared activities, compliments, listening, empathy, acceptance, or emotional space
- Motivate friends and family to do what we want

Self-Mastery
We feel helpless to:

- Establish disciplined habits in fitness, eating, and time management
- Live with integrity, with our habits matching our goals
- Perform our best under pressure
- Create emotional well-being in ourselves

In the space below, list three *specific* things you feel helpless to attain from this person (or, if the problem does not involve a person, describe what you feel helpless to achieve). For example, "My team member won't meet deadlines."

____
____
____
____
____

5. What is the request your feelings are making?

Your negative feelings are a request for change. Write down the request your feelings are making of you. For example, "I need to learn what to say to get him to meet deadlines."

____

____

____

____

What to expect when you open to feelings

When first opening to your feelings, you may feel despair or sadness about events from your past—insensitive parents, unrequited love, or rejections from friends. Or, you may feel intense feelings of inadequacy or failure from career or money mistakes. Because you are new to self-acceptance—and still fear negative feelings because you do not view them as a source of wisdom yet—you may wonder if you are going about the practice of self-acceptance "right." You also may wonder if you are "getting worse" because you are having feelings instead of blocking or suppressing them.

This is the point at which most people abandon listening to themselves, because they are inexperienced in managing feelings. Remember, except in the case of pure loss (where winning is not possible), you cannot expect to heal negative feelings simply by feeling them. You still must give your soul what it is crying out for. You can do this by applying the rest of the *Courage to Win* formula and solving your life challenge.

Are you experiencing genuine feelings, or self-pity?

If you are listening to them, most negative feelings are not overwhelming (nor do they last very long). If you find that your feelings are extraordinarily strong, that they are not going away, and you are not gaining insight into what you feel helpless about, you are probably not touching your genuine feelings yet; you may be stuck in self-pity. Self-pity occurs when we feel indignant because life is "forcing" us to feel rejected, inadequate, afraid, etc. Basically, you are feeling shock and disbelief about your problem because you have not moved out of denial yet. This is typical when we are resisting setbacks and loss.

Self-pity is fine, as long as you do not stay at this stage very long. When you move out of self-pity and understand the true nature of your helplessness, your negative feelings will have done their job. Provided you are making progress with your problem, your negativity will subside.

Self-acceptance is not discussing feelings

Some people, upon learning about the idea of accepting and listening to feelings, mistakenly assume they must *talk* about feelings. To listen to feelings, you must feel them, not necessarily discuss them. Talking about feelings can be a good idea after you have clarity about what you need. Or, you may wish to clarify your feelings with an understanding friend or therapist. However, be wary of talking to others in anger, basically taking revenge on them in the name of accepting your feelings.[33] A wonderful guideline for discussing your feelings is to clarify your request: what do you want from this person? This will keep your communications constructive. *Accountability is about the future; blame is about the past.*

Some feelings are not yours

If you are a particularly empathetic or compassionate person, you can easily sense the fears and sadness of others, especially loved ones. At times, you may not realize that some feelings are not yours. You will know the feelings are not yours because they will be about the suffering of another person. You are mainly feeling their sorrow plus compassion, the desire to alleviate their suffering. If this is happening to you, I suggest you find practical ways to help the person in need. If you help this person, your compassion will soon become manageable.

Final thoughts

To conquer any life problem, we must start with self-acceptance. We cannot reverse our learned helplessness unless we know *exactly what we feel helpless about*. This is called clarity, and it is the first step to winning. We gain clarity through self-acceptance: the ability to experience our feelings. Now that you have clarity about your life problem, you can take action to solve it. Yet, clarity is not enough. You still must motivate yourself to act. This is commitment, and it is the second step to winning.

The Practice of Self-Acceptance: A Summary

1. All problems are confusing at first. When we are not winning in career, money, or relationships, we do not know why, because we have not yet glimpsed our learned helplessness. All we are aware of are the symptoms of our suppressed fears and frustrations—depression, procrastination, addictions, low self-esteem, and unhealthy relationships.
2. To win, we must gain clarity. We must learn exactly what we feel helpless about with respect to our life problem.
3. Self-acceptance is the ability to experience your feelings as they are.
4. Negative feelings are really a request for change. By listening to them, you learn how you need to evolve to fulfill your desires.
5. The opposite of self-acceptance is suppression. Suppression is pushing our thoughts and feelings outside our conscious awareness.
6. When you suppress your feelings, you are saying, "I am better off avoiding my learned helplessness, because this is a problem I cannot handle." This is why when it comes to negative feelings, *What you resist, persist.* Your unhappiness will build in you until you acknowledge the request your soul is making.
7. Self-acceptance will give you clarity by taking you beyond your symptoms to the core of your learned helplessness. Instead of wasting your time on symptoms, you can start dealing with your real problem.
8. Self-acceptance also leads to healing. Once you act on the request your feelings are making, your negative feelings will naturally subside.
9. To cultivate self-acceptance, you should re-train your mind in acceptance, experience your feelings using emotional visualization and chakra work, and identify what your feelings are asking for.

CHAPTER EIGHT

The Practice of Commitment

Honour your desires.

Celine Dion is widely considered one of the top live performers in the world. Having seen the show, I can assure you she is a genius on stage. But she faced a crisis that nearly derailed her singing career. On tour years ago, Celine's voice fell apart, leading her to the best throat doctor in the world. The doctor told her that to protect her voice, she would need to completely change the way she was managing her voice. This meant being silent for three weeks and doing singing exercises for hours each day. Celine's husband and manager, Rene, asked how long it would take to see results. The doctor replied, "You won't notice much for three to five years. In five years, Celine will have a better voice." Rene was dumbfounded. He told Celine that he wouldn't blame her if she quit singing altogether. Five years is too long to work without reward.

But Celine didn't hesitate. She knew genius was within her grasp. After five years of carefully training her voice, she said: "My voice had never felt so flexible and powerful. I'd never gotten so much pleasure out of it. That voice, which I love, is the surest and shortest route between what's inside of me and others."[34] Celine's story embodies commitment: honouring your desires by creating a vision and pursuing it.

The second ingredient in the *Courage to Win* formula is commitment

The purpose of the *Courage to Win* formula is to reverse your learned helplessness so you can defeat any life problem. The first ingredient in the formula is the practice of self-acceptance. Now that you have applied self-acceptance to your problem, you have clarity. You know what you feel helpless to attain—what your soul is asking for.

But, you still must motivate yourself to *act* and pursue your desires. This is commitment, and it is the second step to winning. Commitment is honouring your desires by creating a vision and pursuing it. It is what activates an intense, burning desire to attain what we feel helpless about. Here's why:

Learned helplessness is a giving up response, pure and simple. We believe no matter what we do, we cannot win with this person or goal. As a result, when we have learned helplessness, we try to avoid disappointment instead of pursuing what we want. This is called disowning our desires. We start by pretending that winning doesn't matter. We say things like, "He didn't call, but that's Ok. He's not the man I thought he was." Or, "Rich people are missing the meaning of life." Or, "I didn't get the job, but it required too much overtime anyway." If we disown our desires long enough, we stop *knowing* what we want. This condition is known as self-alienation, and it is certainly not for you.

To win, you must lead your life

To win, you must lead your life by honouring your authentic desires, no matter how risky or hopeless they seem. You ask, "What do I want?" and imagine a perfect outcome for your financial, career, or relationship problem. By creating a vision, you activate an intense, burning desire for what you want. This vision will weaken your helplessness—and dissuade you from trying to avoid disappointment. You trigger the law of attraction in your favour and become a person of action with your problem. Commitment also leads to integrity. When you re-connect to your real desires, you know who you are. Your actions mirror your values, and you live a life of perfect integrity.

What is Commitment?

The film *Rudy* is about a football player whose mission in life is to play for Notre Dame University. Since Rudy is barely 5 feet tall and without a speck of athletic ability, his dream seems unlikely to materialize. Yet Rudy is selected for the team because of his unequivocal commitment to it. Just before putting him on the team, the coach says, "You want on the team pretty bad, don't you?" Rudy replies, "Coach, you have no idea. I'll do anything." Have you ever heard anyone say this...and mean it? When is the last time *you* said it?

Commitment is honouring your desires by creating a vision and pursuing it in the world.

When you pursue your desires, you display healthy self-assertiveness. Self-assertiveness is the ability to express your desires appropriately in the world; it is the conviction that *you matter.*[35] When you approach a problem by asking, "What do I want?", you are saying that you have the right to be happy. Once you have decided that you matter, you go deeper and create a vision for your life problem based on your authentic desires. Your vision inspires you to act and manifest your outcome.

The temptation to disown desires

The opposite of commitment is to disown our desires. When we are not winning, it's tempting to pretend that we don't care about winning. In a naïve bid to avoid disappointment, we disconnect from our desires. In practical terms, we disown our desires by talking ourselves out of what we want. In the extreme, we become hostile to the object of our desire. If we want someone's acceptance, we claim we "don't care about him." If our desire is money, we pretend rich people are "superficial and greedy." If we want our boss's approval, we claim we're "sick of the politics." Here are six specific ways we disown desires:

We deny our need for love or respect, becoming hostile
"My boss told me that I didn't meet his expectations. I'm very hurt—all I can think about is how cruel he was, and when I can quit."

We lack self-assertiveness
"I don't mind looking after the kids every night."

We focus on current limitations, not possibilities
"I've never even allowed myself to think about buying a brand new car—it seems so frivolous."

We stay in activities we dislike
"I'm burned out and want to stop teaching, but I'm good at it, and these students need me."

We give in to fear instead of taking action
"I should call that customer, but he's so difficult."

At first, it makes sense to disown desires that seem out of reach. "There's no point in wanting something I can't have," we reason. The challenge is that disowning desires doesn't work. We never truly relinquish our desires for money, love, fulfilling work, self-esteem, and self-actualization. These desires are the very essence of our existence. To deny them is to deny life itself.

Why Commitment?

We need commitment because desire is the only thing strong enough to overcome helplessness and our efforts to avoid disappointment. Magical things happen when we honour our desires.

Commitment energizes us

Honouring desires energizes us. Consider any desire you have in your life, right now. If it is an authentic desire, it will excite you and fill you with energy. We need this energy to overcome the inertia of learned helplessness. When you create a vision for a life problem based on what you want, you tap into a genuine urge for self-expression. You become intrinsically motivated; you do not need extrinsic rewards such as recognition or money. A world class musician put it best: "I never really did anything I didn't like to do, and I never liked to study. I lived to practice, though, and in college I practiced up to 10 hours per day. I was practicing so much my lips were worn down to a frazzle."[36]

Commitment evolves us

Honouring desires evolves us to new stages. Remember, your current desires represent the next stage in your evolution. What you want, right now, is moving you to the next phase in your development. To attain your desires, you must become a person worthy of them. To win in *career*, you must be a highly competent, results driven person. To win in *finances*, you must transform ideas into the physical realm of money by serving others. To win in *relationships*, you must genuinely love people with compassion, empathy, and generosity. By creating a vision for your problem and pursuing it, you realize a higher self.

When you create a vision, you discover who you are. More than anything else, your desires reveal your true self. Instead of feeling helpless or numb over the problem, you are filled with a sense of purpose.

Commitment activates the law of attraction in your favour

Desire also triggers the law of attraction. The law of attraction says we are a living magnet. When we create a vision and meditate on it, we attract what we want because our mental energy is focused in this direction. We spontaneously draw people and circumstances into our lives that correspond with our vision.[37] There are two caveats, however, on the law of attraction. The first is that the law of attraction is only activated if your vision involves actions you love. The law of attraction is activated by positive energy; it is the *energy* in your desires that makes you a living magnet for what you want. If your vision involves activities you dislike, the law of attraction will not apply. The second caveat is that your vision cannot be based on a need for approval. This is a negative, fear-based motive that will derail your goal with its negative energy.[38]

The bottom line

When we disown a relationship, career, or financial desire, we give in to our helplessness. Not only do we distance ourselves from who we really are, we stay passive in the face of our life problem. Our self-alienation creates an emotional void—a sense of meaninglessness about life—without quite knowing why. The opposite of self-alienation is commitment. Commitment means exposing ourselves to the possibility of disappointment, failure, or loss. This is why we need to honour our desires. By creating a vision based on our authentic self, we gain the motivation we need to take a risk.

The practice of commitment is the path to action. Commitment taps into a genuine urge for self-expression that motivates you to act. You discover who you are and transform yourself into a person of action.

CHAPTER NINE

The Practice of Commitment: The Path to Action

Case Studies

The following case studies show how the practice of commitment—honouring our desires—motivates us to take action on life problems. These case studies are:

"My in-laws are sabotaging my relationship."
"I'm broke."
"I've put off getting a degree for a decade."
"My career has been stalled for four years."
"What is my purpose?"
"I lack discipline."

"My in-laws are sabotaging my relationship."

Although Madison had been dating David for years, his parents objected to their engagement because he was Caucasian and she was Asian. Madison was terribly hurt by their reaction and for months she avoided his parents, saying, "I don't care what they think."

Madison knew that avoiding David's parents was the worst thing she could do. David cherished family above all else. Still, she couldn't motivate herself to attend family functions and start mending the rift. I asked Madison to write five different endings to the following sentence: "If I were five percent more honest about my fears today…." Upon seeing this sentence, Madison wept. She finally let in her desire to be loved by his parents, which she knew David desperately wanted. Madison gathered her courage and wrote:

- I'd admit I want them to love me, not reject me.
- I'd see that my real fear is that he will never marry me.
- I'd stop trying so hard to win his parents' approval.
- I wouldn't be eating so much today!

Overcoming Madison's avoidance:
Honouring her desire for a close family

Madison was pretending that David's parents did not matter to her—when, in fact, she desperately wanted a close extended family. She did this to protect herself from the pain of rejection. Yet disowning her desire was neither authentic nor effective. This simple sentence completion exercise re-connected Madison to her disowned desire for closeness with David's parents. Madison let herself imagine what life would be like if she were closer to David's parents. This vision was much more exciting than the petty satisfaction of pouting or revenge. Finally, she had enough positive motivation to take action.

Madison stopped avoiding David's parents. Instead, she and David met with them and listened patiently to their concerns about a bi-racial marriage. Madison was surprised to learn that what his parents *really* wanted was a voice in the wedding plans. (Usually, when people object to a relationship, it is out of jealousy and a fear of being replaced). This initial meeting was the start of much healing between them. Within a year, David's parents were dancing at their reception with joy.

Accepting our vulnerability

When we feel helpless to get love or respect from someone, we often deny our desire for closeness; it makes us feel too vulnerable. Instead, we do what Madison did: we become hostile to the object of our affection. Hostility may disguise our vulnerability for awhile, but it will never get us the love or respect we want. Hostility leads to avoidance or conflict—neither of which builds trust. *The starting point to success with anyone is admitting that you want his or her love and respect.* This connects you with the joy you could have with this person. When you touch the joy, it erodes your desire to protect yourself. You are now motivated to do what it takes to improve the relationship.

"I'm broke."

Jill, an actress, was deeply in debt. "I was broke, unemployed, and ashamed. I was praying for someone to come and save me from it all," she admitted. "I created the debt with my own ignorance, and lack of commitment to a different outcome." For years, Jill avoided thinking about money. She knew she needed to solve her financial problems, but criticizing herself wasn't motivating her. Only the energy of desire would get her to confront her survival fear.

Overcoming Jill's money struggles: Honouring her desire for self-sufficiency

Jill had never acknowledged a deep-seated need we all have: to be self-sufficient. To shield herself from financial stress and survival fear, she had disconnected from this need. But after years of self-alienation, Jill re-connected with a desire to take care of herself: "I knew I needed to stop spending money and start making money. I allowed myself only the essentials of life: food, lodging, and living expenses. All money went straight to the debt once my bare bones expenses were paid. I got a day job and performed up to eight to ten gigs a week on top of it. I kept up this rhythm for just over a year, and soon I was debt-free—and even managed some savings. I was tired, but I handled it MYSELF. I bought a small key chain as the first purchase for myself, in the shape of a heart. It symbolized that I would never again let myself get into debt, and that I would continue to build on my savings. I am very proud of this."

Focusing on possibilities, not limitations

When we focus on the current reality of a problem such as debt, we disown our desire for money without realizing it. To shift ourselves from a survival to a prosperity consciousness, we must shift our focus from what is to what can be. When Jill shifted her focus from her survival consciousness to taking care of herself (a prosperity consciousness), she transformed her financial life. When focusing on possibilities, we need to live beyond our imagination long enough to dream. Dreaming cripples our helplessness and activates desire at the same time. There is a simple phrase we can use to start the process of dreaming: "Why not me?"

"Why Not Me?"

Mark Tewksbury is one of the finest swimmers ever produced in Canada. The night before his 100 metre backstroke victory at the 1992 Olympics, Mark was feeling the pressure. Suddenly, he had a new thought: "In the field of eight swimmers, only four guys were likely to win. Somebody has to win this race. Why not me?"[39]

"Why not me?" is a beautiful question. Mark wasn't pressuring himself by saying, "I have to win." He was living out of his imagination, which activates the dream. Indeed, when it comes to solving your life problem, why not you?

"I've put off getting a degree for a decade."

Wendy disowned her desire for a degree for over ten years: "After high school my grant was for the local college, not the 'real' university I had set my heart on. Dad made it clear he wanted me close to home. I ended up taking courses I didn't need in a place I didn't want to be. I skipped lessons, missed exams, and procrastinated on assignments. I flunked out, and was too humiliated to tell anyone. It never occurred to me that my reluctance to go to that college played a role in my poor grades."

Overcoming Wendy's fear of failure: Honouring her desire for a degree

Wendy had refused to think about getting a degree. In an effort to avoid the potential disappointment of failure, she simply told herself it didn't matter. But at 30, Wendy finally re-activated her desire: "The thought of going back to University was always at the back of my mind—niggling, pushing, pleading. After that first failure, I wasn't sure I had the intelligence. It took a year to get up my nerve. I was working but arranged to attend just one class, as a try. I promised myself if I achieved a B, I'd keep going. To my surprise, I got an A! I cried. It had been such a long time coming. But there was no stopping me now—I quit my job, got a loan, and enrolled full-time. At long last, I was *in*!"

The power of self-assertiveness

For Wendy, the path to commitment lay in self-assertiveness. Self-assertiveness is the conviction that *you matter*. It is the ability to place your desires first. Growing up, most of us were encouraged to put other peoples' needs before our own. It can be frightening to assert our needs when they contradict what parents, spouses, or authority figures had in mind for us. We were told that a good person is someone who gives, whether giving is in his best interest or not. At work, we say things like, "My job doesn't matter to me. I'm just going to get a job that pays the bills." Then we spend 8 hours a day doing things we don't want to do. At home, we say things like, "I don't care which movie we go to," or "I don't mind doing more than my share of household work." Do not be deceived by the fact that these are small things. If you cannot assert yourself with small things, how will you assert yourself with big things?

Self-assertiveness is a powerful way to honour your desires. The moment you decide *you matter* in any life problem, you free yourself to create a vision based on who you really are. Your vision will spark the energy you need to take action, no matter how much others pressure you.

"My career has been stalled for four years."

Alan is a frustrated information technology executive. "My career has been stalled for close to four years now," he sighed. "My major hurdle is my unwillingness to develop trusting relationships with key colleagues." I asked, "How has this hurt your career?" Alan replied, "I find myself disliking people and focusing on their shortcomings. Although I haven't jumped ship very often in my 25 year career, I have left organizations due to my isolation." I assigned Alan some *Courage to Win* readings on relationships. After careful reflection, he recognized the underlying problem: "I think I resent people because I'm a bit passive at work. I don't ask for support; I avoid conflict at all costs, and I let my colleagues control meetings. I also do work that should have been done by others." I didn't speak. Alan was on a roll: "I'm passive with them so I can gain their acceptance. But, I actually set the relationship up for failure. When I over-accommodate people, I resent them and eventually withdraw from the relationship."

**Overcoming Alan's passiveness:
Honouring his desire for a team at work**

Alan desperately wanted his team to pull their weight. Yet for years, he had told himself not to "rock the boat" by asking subordinates to do their jobs. He'd think, "It's not worth a fight. I'd rather do it myself." To motivate himself to make requests, Alan had to tap into his heart-felt need for a team willing to help him. Fortunately, Alan knew the joy of "team." He completely trusted his family, and was assertive with them. He routinely made requests that his wife and children agreed to. Alan visualized how exciting work could be if he could create a similar team there. The very next week, he told me, "I've already started asking for what I need at work. For me, this is a whole new level of commitment to team. I'm excited about moving forward."

There are three ways of communicating: passively, aggressively, and assertively. Passivity means saying nothing about our desires. Aggressiveness means overpowering others with our desires. Assertiveness means asking for what we need in an appropriate way. If we want to be a leader at home or work, we must be comfortable making requests.

"What is my purpose?"

Jacob was confused about his career. A successful speaker on time management, Jacob loved the subject, but something was missing. He felt anxious before his presentations and exhausted after them. Jacob liked people, but he was introverted, and being with them constantly sapped his energy.

Jacob knew he needed a change. He also knew that his career procrastination was making him miserable. But when he tried to brainstorm a new career, he felt lost. "I really don't know what my purpose is. I've thought and thought, but nothing comes to mind. What now?" he asked me.

Overcoming Jacob's self-alienation: Honouring his desire to organize the company

Jacob had taken jobs others had proposed to him for so long that he had lost touch with his own desires. To discover who Jacob really was, he needed to go back to the beginning. I suggested that Jacob write down activities that made him happy at every age. It was an easy list for him to generate:

1. Kicking a ball against a wall at recess
2. Shooting hoops in his driveway
3. Organizing and cleaning his room
4. Being alone at his family's cabin (doing puzzles, reading, fishing)

Next, I asked Jacob, "What appealed to you about these activities at their core?" After some reflection, he replied, "They all involve mastery and solitude. I'm basically a geek. I like working alone, I love organizing, and I need to see tangible results right away." These were the types of activities that filled Jacob with energy. They were his true life's purpose. However, Jacob harboured a secret fear of selling—particularly selling himself. This fear had perpetuated his self-alienation: if he pursued what he really wanted to do, he'd have to confront his helplessness over selling his services.

For years, Jacob had suppressed his interest in a different role to avoid the rejection of pursuing his dream job. To overcome the fear of rejection, Jacob harnessed the power of desire. He sat down and wrote out a role perfectly suited to his skills and temperament, that of an internal consultant who would organize and streamline the company's business processes. This vision filled Jacob with excitement—enough to kick start him into action. It didn't take Jacob long to secure a new role in his company. Instead of teaching, he became the guy-behind-the-guy, creating the firm's business processes. Jacob relished the solitude of his office. He loved creating order, and saw changes virtually overnight.

What makes your heart sing at work?

When Jacob focused on the activities that intrinsically motivated him, he took himself to a new level of commitment. Many people get paralyzed over career options. They assume they need a glamorous job to be fulfilled. To be fulfilled, glamour is not necessary, but finding your highest self at work is. You may excel at many tasks, but only a few will make your heart sing. How do you know which activities make your heart sing? They flood you with energy. They put you in the zone, the zen moment, the Now. When engaged in them, you are neither self-seeking nor self-conscious. You are responding to what the moment demands. You are not constantly seeking praise, nor are you motivated solely by recognition or profit. The activity itself is its own joy, because it causes you to delight in your abilities.[40]

When you discover the activities that make your heart sing, learned helplessness will never get the best of you. No matter how many setbacks you encounter, you will find a way to engage in these activities more often.

"I lack discipline."

When Darren came to see me, he had hit rock bottom over his divorce. He was so depressed over the loss that he was having trouble reporting for work each day. I asked him to write an essay on a time when he had been exceptionally disciplined. When Darren came back with the essay, he seemed lighter; his despair had lifted a little.

Darren admitted: "When you asked me to write about discipline, I wasn't sure I had any. But I was the top salesman in my company for years. So I asked myself, 'Why was I the #1 guy every year?' Finally it hit me: I was the only guy who *always* asked the client to buy. I'd say: "Mr. Prospect, I've answered all your questions and addressed all your concerns. Now, I want your business." Then I'd give him the contract to sign...and wait. Sometimes it was a full two minutes before he did anything. During those two minutes, my anxiety skyrocketed. It never got easy to ask for the order. But I did it anyway. The other sales guys only asked for the order 85% of the time. But I *always* asked for it. I guess my biggest strength is discipline. I ask for the sale, whether I want to or not."

Darren had been so caught up in the trauma of his divorce that his inner game (his feelings) were completely dominating his outer game (actions). To gain some control back into his life, Darren needed to invoke discipline.

Developing discipline: Outer game comes *before* inner game

Discipline is your ability to separate your actions from your feelings. Your *outer game* is your actions. Your *inner game* is your feelings. When you are disciplined, you habitually place your outer game before your inner game. You take action to solve your problem, whether you feel like it or not.

Every problem requires a little discipline. On some days, no matter how diligent we are at tapping into our desires, learned helplessness or loss can make us a little passive. If we are disciplined enough to keep taking action despite our helplessness, good things will happen. With each little success, desire is re-born, and our motivation is restored.

CHAPTER TEN

Cultivating the Practice of Commitment:

Action Steps

Here are five action steps you can use to apply commitment to any problem. Please apply these steps to the personal challenge you are working on.

1. Develop self-assertiveness

To start, I want you to decide that *your desires matter* with respect to the relationship, money, or career problem you are facing. Here is a practical exercise to accomplish this. First, keep your life challenge in mind when you complete this exercise. Next, generate five different endings for the following sentence each day: "If I were 5% more self-assertive today...." Here are some sample endings:

- I'd talk more instead of just listening to my sister
- I'd ask my boss for more responsibility at work
- I'd tell my husband I hate hiking
- I'd ask my friends to go to the restaurant of my choice
- I'd take piano lessons instead of taking my kids sailing

Complete this exercise every day for two weeks. Gradually, you will come to see which desires you are subordinating with respect to your challenge and how you can express them in an appropriate way.

2. What is your desired outcome?

To solve any life problem, you must know what you want. What is the ideal outcome for your problem? This is the technique of goal-setting, and it is a powerful method for re-connecting to your authentic desires. Remember, this is a time to focus on possibilities, not current limitations. You can use Donald Trump's motto: "I like thinking big. I always have. To me it's very simple: if you're going to be thinking anyway, you might as well think big."[41] I am asking you to select only one goal so you can develop commitment with respect to a single problem. Of course, once you hammer in a nail, you don't throw out the hammer. You will use the practice of commitment throughout your life to realize your deepest aspirations.

Make sure your goal is specific. This will ensure a direct path to success.

Examples of non-specific goals:	Examples of specific goals:
1. I want to be happier in my job.	1. I want to get a professorship position in a University.
2. I want to gain confidence in my knowledge and abilities.	2. I want to express my ideas in meetings at least twice per week.
3. I want more balance in my life.	3. I want to improve my efficiency at work so I am working a maximum of 50 hours per week.
4. I want to figure out my career.	4. I want to change fields and become a full-time journalist.
5. I want my boss to give me added responsibility.	5. I want to become a project manager in my department.
6. Now that I am divorcing, I need a career that will pay enough so I can continue to live in my home.	6. I want to make $100,000 this year without increasing my hours.
7. I want to enhance my communication skills at work.	7. I want to deliver moving, entertaining speeches to large groups.

8. I want my boss to respect me.	8. I want my boss to seek out my opinions at our weekly meeting.
9. I want to stop resenting my mother so much.	9. I want to assert myself with my mother and not allow her to bully me.
10. I want to be less lonely.	10. I want to reconcile with my spouse.
11. I want a better relationship with my daughter.	11. I want my daughter to listen to me with empathy.

You will know when you have set the right goal—the one that is the antidote to your problem—because the moment you write it down, the goal will excite you.

Set your goal here:

____
____
____
____
____

Set a sub-goal *under your control*

To complement your major goal, set a sub-goal that is under your direct and immediate control. This is one of the critical lessons about winning that sport has taught us. In sport, the only way you can win (achieve the performance goal) is by focusing on a goal under your control (a process goal).

In the 2000 Olympics, I watched U.S. track star Marion Jones warming up for her first race, the 200 metre. As the cameras zeroed in on Jones, the announcer turned to Olympic sprinter Michael Johnson and said, "All eyes are focused on Marion. *What* is going through her mind right now?" The camera panned to Michael. Politely he replied, "Well, I'd imagine she's thinking about how to get a good start out of the blocks." An elite athlete himself, Michael knew that Marion's best focus would NOT be on the outcome of the race. The only way she could win would be to focus on a goal *under her control,* such as how to get a clean start out of the blocks. The 200 metre is a short race. If you get a good start, and you're Marion Jones, you're going to win. Here are some examples of goals under your control:

- I will read one book this week on how to deliver moving anecdotes in presentations.
- I will ask my boss if there is anything I can do to ease his workload or stress.
- I will call my broker and review my investments with him.
- I will listen with understanding when my daughter talks about school.

Set a sub-goal under your control here:

____

____

____

____

____

3. Visualize your desired outcome

Visualizing your desired outcome triggers intense, burning desire for what you want. This positive emotion inspires you to act and triggers the law of attraction in your favour. Here is a potent visualization sequence you can apply to your life challenge:

Breathe easily and slowly. Feel the relaxation spread through your body... down through your face, your neck, your solar plexus, and your feet. You are feeling calm and wonderful about yourself. Continue to breathe deeply and relax.

I want you to remember a time in your life when you felt powerful, confident, and successful. Bring the event that triggers these feelings forward in your mind. See it clearly, and connect to these feelings. Let yourself have them.

Now run this event in your mind. What are you wearing? Who is there with you? Where are you? Run through your accomplishment in your mind. Let it serve as a model for your current goal. Let yourself have the feelings of confidence and joy this event evokes in you.

Now, project yourself forward through space and time. Imagine that your current goal is a reality. Take yourself through the specifics of this goal. What are you wearing? Who is there with you? What performance are you having? How are people responding to you?

Let yourself have all the positive feelings associated with this goal–feelings of pride, joy, and success. Breathe into these feelings. Have a sense of gratitude that you are able to bring about this result. Now, gently, open your eyes and smile. You will carry the joy of this goal with you throughout the day.

What to expect when visualizing

As you access your positive emotions, suppressed negative feelings may jump out at you. For example, if you imagine and see yourself being really successful in your goal, you may have feelings of self-doubt: *Can I keep up this success*?, shame: *Do I deserve this*?, or insignificance: *Is this all there is?* These feelings are probably residue from previous disappointments with your challenge. Or, they might be a request from your soul to learn new skills that will help you succeed. These are all natural responses to this exercise; do not be deterred by anything negative that erupts. Simply listen to what these feelings may be asking you for—training, new skills, better preparation, etc.

When Olympic swimmer Mark Tewksbury first started visualizing, he had his share of frustrations: "When I first started [visualizing], it was frustrating and exhausting. I would close my eyes and try to picture the race and nothing would come. Sometimes I fell asleep instead of visualizing. Other times all I could see were my competitors. Even worse, sometimes when I had pictured myself doing well, I would get in the race and panic when the first little thing didn't go according to plan.[42]

Or, you may not feel anything at all. You may be able to see the image but not access any feelings. You may get in touch with a positive feeling—pride, joy, or confidence—and then lose it quickly.

Be patient with yourself. These are all perfectly normal experiences with visualization; it is a skill that needs practice to be perfected. Do not try to force anything. Continue to return to the positive images in your mind. If there are negative feelings, allow them to break through and run their course. If you experience them without resistance using self-acceptance, you will know what this negativity is telling you. As you repeat this exercise, feelings of confidence, joy, and success about your vision will become easier to sustain.

4. Focus on possibilities using optimism

As you formulate your action plan for your life problem, you can use optimism to keep yourself moving forward when learned helplessness rears its ugly head. A core tenant of optimism is the conviction that your problem is *temporary*. This is called hope, and it is the stuff of champions. Optimism is not positive thinking. Positive thinking means finding a silver lining (something good) about a setback. For example, if you lose a client, being positive is saying, "I'm glad I lost that client because I didn't have the time to manage his account anyway."

Optimism is different. One element of optimism is *finding a legitimate reason to believe a setback is temporary.*[43] For example, if you lose a client, being optimistic is saying, "I'm disappointed I lost a client. However, I fixed the problem that made him angry. I believe I will retain all my other clients, and maybe win him back."

Through optimism, you plant the suggestion in your mind that by taking new, effective action, *it is possible for you to attain your vision.* I call this the Muhammad Ali strategy. Ali was famous for psyching himself up using unparalleled optimism. Ali, considered the most successful athlete of the past 100 years, would tell anyone who'd listen that he was going to win. However, you don't need to become outwardly boastful the way Ali was. ☺ It's sufficient to use optimism in the privacy of your own mind. In fact, psychologists have discovered that by repeating the simple phrase "*I can do it,*" you create hope very quickly.

In *Learned Optimism: How to Change Your Mind and Your Life*, Martin Seligman provides a practical, simple method for cultivating optimistic thinking when you need it. Here it is:

To begin, write down your fears about your personal challenge in the left hand column. This will reveal the unconscious learned helplessness you are holding about it. Then, in the right hand column, write down legitimate suggestions about why these setbacks could be temporary. [Note: make sure your suggestions are realistic. Otherwise, they will not inspire hope in you.]

I have completed some sample thoughts for you to use as models. Note that the optimistic response does not try to find something good in the situation; it simply provides a rational explanation for why the setback is temporary.[44]

Goal/Desire	Pessimistic Thought	Optimistic Thought
I want to secure an Executive position in the insurance industry.	My sales skills are inadequate for this role.	I can spend time with my mentor, Phil, and apply an hour per day studying it.
Goal/Desire	**Pessimistic Thought**	**Optimistic Thought**
I want to get to know Jim.	He's not interested in me.	I owe it to myself to find out. I can attract him if I learn what he needs in a relationship.
Goal/Desire	**Pessimistic Thought**	**Optimistic Thought**

Note: at this point, you might be tempted to worry about the nuts-and-bolts strategies you need to learn in order to defeat your challenge. Do not worry about this issue yet—we will cover it in the practice of competence. In the meantime, I assure you that you will learn the technical skills and know-how to solve your problem.

5. Invoke discipline

Discipline is essential if you want to translate your goal into everyday terms. Here are three planning steps you can use to invoke discipline with respect to your goal:

1. Set a deadline to achieve your major goal. For example: I will apply to 15 Universities within the next month.
2. Set deadlines for your sub goals that are under your control (everything you need to do in order to achieve the goal). Keep evolving your list and deadlines as you make progress.

3. Take action on your plan today. Do something every day to move you towards your outcome *whether you want to act or not.*

If you have a bad day, listen to your feelings using self-acceptance—but do not let them deter you from acting. When dealing with complex life problems, sometimes our feelings lag behind our intentions. We want to act, but still feel a little pessimistic. The beauty of our outer game—our actions—is that we can control them. You can start solving your problem today, whether you feel like it or not.

Final thoughts

Commitment, the drive to act and improve our circumstances, is our natural state. Yet, when learned helplessness strikes, commitment eludes us. We become more focused on avoiding disappointment than winning. To rescue our motivation, we need a vision based on our authentic desires. When it comes to any life problem, we must ask, "What do I want?"

Honouring our desires empowers us by tapping into our authentic passion for what we want. The positive energy of desire restores our motivation to act and outweighs our need to avoid risk. Yet, not all actions are created equal. To win, you must take effective action. This brings us to the final practice of mental toughness in the *Courage to Win* formula: the practice of competence.

The Practice of Commitment: A Summary

1. Having applied self-acceptance to your problem, you now have clarity. You know what you feel helpless to attain. But, you still must motivate yourself to *act* and solve your life problem.
2. Motivating ourselves to act when we have learned helplessness is not easy. When we're not winning, we're tempted to disown our desires. This creates self-alienation: we do not know what we want.
3. The practice of commitment is honouring your desires by creating a vision and pursuing it in the world.
4. To honour your desires, you ask, "What do I want?" and imagine a perfect outcome for your financial, career, or relationship

problem. By creating a vision, you activate a burning desire for what you want, which weakens your helplessness.

5. By tapping into our authentic desires, we energize and evolve ourselves. We also trigger the law of attraction in our favour.
6. We honour desires by accepting our vulnerability to others. Instead of becoming hostile to affection, we need to admit our desire for love, respect, or affection from this person. This will motivate us to do what it takes to improve the relationship.
7. Honouring desires requires focusing on possibilities instead of limitations. Top performers live out of their imagination long enough to dream pass current realities. The excitement of your dream will cripple your helplessness and encourage you to take a risk.
8. Honouring desires requires self-assertiveness. Self-assertiveness is the conviction that your desires matter. When you decide that *you matter*, you pursue what you want despite pressure from others.
9. By discovering which activities that make your heart sing at work, you tap into a genuine desire for self-expression that is intrinsically motivating.
10. A final way to honour your desires is through discipline. Discipline is the ability to put your outer game (actions) above your inner game (feelings). You do what you know you should do, whether you feel like it or not.
11. To apply the practice of commitment to a problem, you use sentence completions for self-assertiveness, goal-setting, visualization, optimism, and discipline.

CHAPTER ELEVEN

THE PRACTICE OF COMPETENCE

THE FUTURE BELONGS TO THE COMPETENT.

Years ago, a reporter accosted golf legend Jack Nicklaus and told him golf was primarily a game of luck, not skill. Jack replied, "Yeah, and the funny thing is, the more I practice, the luckier I get." Jack knew what all top performers know: To win, we need superior technique.

The third ingredient in the *Courage to Win* formula is competence

The third ingredient in the *Courage to Win* formula is competence. Competence is having superior technique. There are proven success principles in money, relationships, and career. When you learn and internalize them, you develop superior technique. This is competence, and it is the third step to winning. At this stage in applying the *Courage to Win* formula, you have a goal: a desired outcome for your problem. You are also motivated to act. However, not all actions are created equal. To win, you must take *effective* action.

Few people train themselves long enough to discover how good they can truly be. When we have learned helplessness, we rarely focus on competence. Our conviction that "nothing we do will make a difference" creates passivity, not ambition. If we don't know *how* to solve a problem, we tend to a) assume it's unsolvable or b) blame others. We say things like, "There's no point in talking to him, he won't listen." Or, "Cash flow is tight, but small business is always a struggle." Or, "It's too late to make a career change now." If we rationalize our poor results by pretending we have nothing to learn—or by blaming—it never occurs to us to acquire new skills. This phenomenon is pride, and it is the main obstacle to competence.

To win, you need superior technique

If you are not winning in relationships, career, or money, someone on this earth has the solution to your problem. You must swallow your pride and find that solution. This means assuming you "don't know what you don't know" and finding the right source to help you. Too often, our pride keeps us paralyzed. We want to believe we already have the answers. Jerry Seinfeld says pride is why so many bookstores have trouble attracting customers: "A bookstore is a 'smarter than you' store. And that's why people are intimidated—because to walk into a bookstore, you have to admit there's something you don't know."[45] When you apply the practice of competence to your problem, you drop your pride in favour of humility. Somewhere deep inside, you realize that you can learn more about how to win in relationships, career, and money. Through mentors, coaching, reading and practice, you develop superior technique. Your newfound skill gives you confidence, which dissolves the last shreds of learned helplessness in your mind. Now that you know *how* to win, you believe you *can* win.

What is Competence?

Competence is having superior technique.

Whether you are parenting your five-year-old, playing the violin, performing heart surgery, selling advertising, or trying to get a date, there is no substitute for superior technique.

Edwin Moses is the most accomplished hurdler in the history of track and field. He won the 400 metre hurdles for ten years. For ten years, he didn't lose a race. Primarily, it was because he was the only guy in the world who could take 13 steps between hurdles (instead of 14). He just had superior technique.[46] When you have superior technique, you understand tiny nuances that no one else sees. Hank Aaron, long-time holder of the Major League Baseball record for home runs, had a unique hitting approach. Unlike most hitters, who worried about batting form, Aaron focused on the pitcher. Aaron didn't worry about his hands or his hips. Instead, he would think, "What is good for Koosman, what works for Koosman, and how is he going to try and get me out?"[47] The concept of superior technique applies in all domains of life: money, relationships, and career. Donald Trump is an example of superior technique in real estate development and deal-making.

"Deals are my art form."

Trump learned the art of deal-making at home. From the time he could walk, he went to construction sites with his father. He learned how to handle contractors, real estate salespeople, and bankers. By the time Trump moved from Queens to Manhattan in New York, he already had an advantage over every up-and-coming real estate developer: first hand experience from his father's business. Eventually, Trump became one of the most skilled tycoons in the country. He says: "Other people paint beautifully on canvas. I like making deals, preferably big deals. Deals are my art form."[48]

The opposite of competence is mediocre technique

The opposite of competence is mediocre technique. The truth is, most of us have mediocre technique in everything—sales, making money, communication, leadership, financial literacy, performing under pressure, triggering attraction in lovers, parenting, time management, running a business—the list goes on. It is a rare person who has the objectivity to grasp this and make a serious commitment to competence.

"I'd never do that much work."

As a teenager, I wanted to be competent in my sport, ringette. When I was 18, I put together an elaborate binder that included:

- A 21 page essay on how I could improve my skills
- Monthly, weekly and daily fitness regimens
- Goals for shooting sessions and practices
- Mental toughness training strategies

The binder was my sports "Bible" until I reached my goal of being named captain of Team Canada ten years later. I kept my binder a secret until a talented young player asked me for help making the National Team. She studied it and finally confessed, "It looks great, but to be honest, I'd never do that much work."

Why Competence?

We need competence because it is central to winning. There are two reasons for this. First, to solve complex life problems, it is not enough to clarify our helplessness (self-acceptance) and motivate ourselves to act (commitment). Money, career, and relationships all have a performance element. To succeed in any one of these areas, we need superior technique in the following:

Money

1. You must know how to make money. Usually, this involves knowing how to sell (either a product to customers or your services to an employer).
2. You must know how to create or invest in financial assets that make money for you.
3. You must become financially literate—with enough savvy to navigate investments, loans, and taxes.

Career

1. You must choose the right career for *you.*
2. You must be highly competent in your technical area (engineering, accounting, sales, etc.)
3. You must know how to get along with others, including how to motivate them.
4. You must be productive with your time.
5. You must know how to perform well under pressure.

Love & Friendship

1. You must know how to attract lovers, spouses, and friends.

2. You must know how to inspire people to give you physical affection, time in shared activities, compliments, listening, empathy, acceptance, or emotional space.
3. You must know how to motivate friends and family to cooperate with you.

The more competent you are in all these areas, the more successful you will be. The second reason competence leads to winning is that it is much easier to defeat learned helplessness when we learn superior technique. When we have superior technique, we instantly spark hope. The following is an example of how competence dissolves helplessness and restores hope to a painful life problem.

Stop your divorce

The book *Stop Your Divorce* tells the story of a man (we'll call him Luke), who was distraught because his wife kept saying, "I don't love you any more. I want a divorce." He sought help from a therapist with 45 years' experience reconciling couples. This therapist told Luke *exactly* what to say the next time his wife asked for a divorce. The next day, Luke called back his therapist, very excited. He said: "She came home said that she didn't love me and she wanted a divorce. I told her what you told me to say. She got up, walked around the house for five minutes, then returned to the bedroom and said, "You know, I think this marriage CAN work. And I want it to work."

What Luke Said

When his wife told him she wanted a divorce, Luke said three simple things:

1. "You're right. Our marriage will never work."
2. "I would prefer to stay married, but you're not happy."
3. "I'll look for an apartment next week."

Before this, Luke used to argue with her and tell her why they should stay together. This would irk her, and an argument would follow.

Why Luke's Approach Worked

1. Luke agreed with his wife instead of arguing. Most people relax their position when you agree with them and defend their position when you argue with them.
2. Luke listened to her, which made her feel she was being understood.
3. Luke told her that he preferred to stay married to her, placing the responsibility for the divorce solely on her. Since there are usually many good elements in a marriage, neither partner wants to be completely responsible for ending it.
4. Luke showed he wasn't afraid to be alone, which demonstrated his personal confidence. Confidence is universally attractive, and fear is universally unattractive.[49]

By using superior technique in communication skills, Luke got his wife to open up a little. Now he can find out *why* she wants a divorce, which is necessary for a reconciliation. Luke's story is an example of how powerful superior technique can be in reversing learned helplessness and turning around a life problem.

The cornerstones of competence: humility and accountability

The practice of competence starts with humility. Humility is recognizing you "don't know what you don't know" and deciding to learn.

A leader humble enough to succeed

Years ago I worked with a Finnish ringette coach named Junnu whose team had terrible mood swings. They'd dominate the first period, lose the second period, then battle back in the third. He asked me, "How can I help the team be more consistent?" I watched his team, and he was right. After controlling the first period, they fell behind in the second, and scrambled to tie it up in the third. After the game, I asked him, "What motivates your team?" Junnu's mind went completely blank. He'd been coaching these athletes for four years, yet didn't know *one thing* that motivated them. I quickly asked, "What *doesn't* motivate your team?

This time, he came up with one idea: "Yelling. Yelling at them doesn't work." (Of course, yelling was the only thing he had been doing). Junnu's saving grace was humility. He acknowledged his lack of awareness about his team and decided to stop yelling and learn. After that day, Junnu watched his athletes carefully, making notes on what they liked (and didn't like) about his coaching. He found that compliments were the only thing that consistently motivated them.

Two years later, Junnu's team was poised to win the National Championship. He gathered the team and said, "You are so ready to win this game. I mean, look who we have in this room." One by one, he complimented each player: "Kirsi, you're the ultimate buzzsaw on the ice, checking every player who skates near you." Chills went up and down the players' spines as they absorbed his praise. You may have guessed that Junnu's team won. You're right. To this day, Junnu still talks about the power of humility.

Focus on what you can control

Humility is one cornerstone of competence. The other is personal accountability. When we are focused on blame, we obsess about the person or situation that has upset us, instead of developing superior technique. Competence means dropping blame and focusing on our own actions, regardless of the problem we are facing. Winning involves an important paradox: the moment we stop spending energy on things we cannot control and re-invest it in actions we *can* control, we begin to win. And the only thing we can directly control is our actions. Fortunately, action is powerful. Superior technique will create breakthroughs in even the toughest problems.

The bottom line

The practice of competence gives you the skills of a winner. Instead of wallowing in arrogance or blame, you get busy learning proven success principles in money, career, and relationships. As your competence grows, so does your confidence, and your learned helplessness fades away. Soon, you've solved your life problem, and moved on to the next one. Before long, nothing can stop you.

CHAPTER TWELVE

THE PRACTICE OF COMPETENCE:

THE PATH TO EFFECTIVENESS

The following case studies show how competence enhances effectiveness. By applying the practice of competence to their life problems, these individuals achieved major breakthroughs. These case studies are:

"The men I like are commitment-shy, but I don't like the men who want me."
"My staff resists tasks."
"I want to be wealthy, not just comfortable."
"My boss won't listen."
"I'm afraid of choking under pressure."

Note: In these case studies, I will reveal several proven success principles in relationships, money, and career. Please pay special attention to situations that resemble your personal challenge.

"The men I like are commitment-shy, but I don't like the men who want me."

There was no doubt about it, Brooke was unlucky in love. She fell in love with men who wouldn't commit, yet didn't like the men who wanted her. All Brooke's relationships started out the same way. At first, everything would be perfect: they would share intense lovemaking, romance, and total understanding of each other. Within a few months, however, Brooke would become the pursuer, wanting more and more connectedness and feeling less and less satisfied. As her lover pulled away, Brooke would start fights, causing him to withdraw. Finally, Prince Charming would fade away completely, leaving her bitter and confused.

Mediocre technique in keeping attraction alive

Brooke was not winning in love because she had mediocre technique in keeping attraction alive in a relationship. Brooke did not understand the *pursuit dynamic* in relationships. Here is what I shared with her.

The Pursuit Dynamic

In every relationship, one person is more in touch with the need for connectedness (the pursuer), while the other is more in touch with the need for independence (the pursuee). If you are the pursuer, you tend to want more time, more listening, more affection, and more intimacy. If you are the pursuee, you tend to want less conversation, less time together, and less intimacy. This dynamic applies in all types of relationships: lovers, spouses, friends, family members, and colleagues.

The pursuit dynamic is the first one to show itself in every relationship. It is also the dynamic that governs attraction between two people. If the pursuit dynamic is reasonably balanced at the beginning, the relationship has a chance of lasting. Otherwise, it will die a quick and painful death. If the pursuit dynamic is not managed well, it becomes unbalanced. When this happens, most people will do one of two things:

1. If you are the pursuer, you will over-pursue. Without realizing it, you will pressure the other person for more connection, affection or respect, causing him to her to withhold it. Over-pursuers are often female.

2. If you are the pursuee, you will feel suffocated and avoid connecting. The other person is pressuring you for more connection, affection, or respect, and this triggers negativity in you. People who avoid connecting are often male.

Here are some examples of over-pursuing:

At home

- You call too often (and don't realize it).
- You wait around for people instead of making your own plans.
- You call people and tell them you're lonely or depressed.
- You are overly doting, leaving them no room to come your way.
- You agree to spend time with a person when it's inconvenient.
- You are having a bad time with a person, but instead of politely ending your time with him or her, you stay in the situation.
- You give affection even when the other person isn't being affectionate.
- You stop being focused on your life and focus on the other person.
- You ask for re-assurance about your personality, looks, etc.

At work

- You stop by colleagues' desks to socialize, even when they are busy.
- You run every decision (even tiny ones) by your boss for fear of mistakes.
- You over-report on your activities to gain re-assurance.
- You micro-manage employees by unnecessarily checking up on them.
- You over-explain your decisions when feeling inadequate.
- You make sarcastic remarks about things that aren't getting done instead of asking for them directly.
- You share inappropriate information about your personal life.

Over-pursuing is a relationship mistake that few people will notice on their own. It is perhaps the greatest barrier to getting the love, friendship, or respect you want. When you are over-pursuing, you are plagued with feelings of frustration, rejection and abandonment. Consciously and unconsciously, you will *blame* the person you are pursuing for not responding. (If you are the pursuee, you will feel suffocated, annoyed, and guilty for not being able to respond to the pursuer). If you are the pursuer, you will frequently pursue more in an attempt to get the person to give you more time, affection, respect, and love. Here's how it shows up: you will become extremely pleasant and flexible in an attempt to please and win over the person. Every now and again, when frustrated, you'll become critical, accusing the pursuee of being insensitive, unappreciative, or not giving enough. You may complain or lay guilt trips: "You don't appreciate me." Or, exhausted from the pursuit, you may give up and abandon the relationship thinking, "You can't change another person," or "He's emotionally unavailable."

Over-pursuing is a typical response when we are being rejected. However, over-pursuing does not work to create closeness between two people. It does not work because it violates a basic law of attraction in life: *any person pursued runs away*.

Psychological leaning

Taken by itself, pursuit is not wrong or destructive. Pursuing for connection is part of every relationship. It is *over-pursuing* that is the problem. How do you know when you have crossed into over-pursuing? It is when you over-pursue to avoid a negative feeling: fear, rejection, insecurity, inadequacy, insignificance, or loneliness. When your desire to connect is driven by fear, you are less likely to notice another person's need for space. You will pressure him or her, and this never works. No one wants to absorb your fears; no one wants his need for independence ignored.

This is why people do not respond to being over-pursued. It is a form of pressure, and we all react against pressure. This is called *psychological leaning*.[50] In *Silent Power*, Stuart Wilde explains why psychological leaning repels people: "When you lean psychologically or emotionally on people or towards them, it makes others feel uncomfortable. They resent the weight you are laying on them, and they will react by denying you. They don't like your self-indulgence, and your insecurity reminds them of their own vulnerability; it rattles them. Animosity builds. Consciously and subliminally, they sense the weakness your leaning creates. It robs them of energy and crowds them; they have to buy into your needs and emotions when they would prefer to concentrate on their own. They don't like the imposition, and often they react negatively, even if they don't say so. Alternatively, they accept the imposition of your weight, but then they feel they can take advantage of you emotionally, sexually, or financially. They will feel empowered to use you or deprecate you or discredit you in some way."[51]

You lean on someone psychologically when you use your connection with them to gain confidence or self-acceptance. On some level, you want this person to calm your fears.

Brooke: Balancing the pursuit dynamic

I explained to Brooke that the quickest way for her to balance the pursuit cycle is to stop over-pursuing her boyfriend through her words and actions. This does not mean being hostile towards him. She can be responsive, friendly, and even affectionate. She simply stops pursuing, which means not initiating contact or intimacy; she also stops pressuring him to be any different than he is right now.

You accept what he is giving, and you appreciate it. (Note: I am not talking about a situation in which one person is being verbally or physically abusive to another). When you appreciate what you are getting from another person, he or she tends to give you more. Here are some basic guidelines to use in balancing out the pursuit dynamic:

1. Let him initiate contact. Respond to his calls, but do not initiate contact. Contact him once time for every few times he contacts you.
2. Make pleasant conversation about fun, interesting topics—nothing heavy. Rarely discuss the status of the relationship unless he does; and when he does, listen to him.
3. Never criticize, complain, or lay a guilt trip on him for not giving you more attention or affection.[52]

Brooke was courageous enough to drop blame and focus on her own behaviour. She followed the guidelines on balancing out the pursuit dynamic religiously. After two months, to Brooke's surprise, her boyfriend was calling more and more often. The new balance in the relationship gave Brooke the freedom to initiate closeness with him regularly. After a few more months, she was able to initiate contact and spontaneous affection without triggering any anxiety in her boyfriend. Eventually, the relationship had excellent balance, and became fun, spontaneous and relaxed.*

"My staff resists tasks."

Cal got frustrated when his new marketing coordinator kept "forgetting" to update the company website. Cal had made several requests for her to complete these updates, yet the coordinator seemed to be ignoring him. "I've made it clear this is part of her job," he sighed. "What more can I do? Reprimand her? I don't want to have conflict so soon after hiring her."

Mediocre technique in overcoming employees' task resistance

For the most part, Cal was a good supervisor. He was comfortable making requests of his team and took great pains to clarify his expectations. Yet when it came to overcoming his staff's resistance to tasks, Cal had mediocre technique. Instead of confronting the issue, he would seethe with resentment, assuming the employee was "lazy," or "had a bad attitude." I explained to Cal that when someone resists a task, there is usually a good reason—*at least in the employee's mind.* As a supervisor, it is Cal's job to uncover and address this reason. This is called uncovering the resistance, and it is central to gaining cooperation from employees, colleagues, and even family.

How to uncover task resistance

In *Nice On My Feelings*, Dr. Terry Orlick tells the story of Little Mary, who wanted to wear her sandals to a picnic. The problem was that Mary's mother wanted her to wear running shoes, not sandals. When Mary's

---

*If you are the person being pursued in a relationship, there are different moves you can make that will balance the pursuit dynamic. When you are the pursuee, you can help balance the dynamic by pursuing the other person more; however, because you are suffering from feelings of suffocation, anxiety, and annoyance, this is difficult to do. You are also not motivated to improve the relationship, because the other person is annoying you. For more coaching on this issue, I recommend my training program, The Courage to Win: Mental Toughness for Success 30 Day LIVE Coaching Program. For details, go to http://www.thecouragetowin.com/coachingprogram.html

mother found that Mary had put on her sandals (and on the wrong feet, yet) she said, "They're on the wrong feet–change into your running shoes." Mary replied, "It doesn't matter." Finally the mom got mad and yelled, "I don't want to spend all morning getting shoes on. I want to go on the picnic," slamming her hand hard on the floor. Mary began to cry and ran towards her room. Her mom intercepted Mary, slid her onto her knee and changed her shoes to the correct feet. She said, "I don't want to hear any more whining or crying," and quickly exited the house with Mary. The next day Dr. Orlick asked Mary why she liked wearing her sandals better than her running shoes. Mary said, "Because I can tie these up, all by myself." Mary wanted to wear shoes under her control, especially since she would be taking them on and off all day at the picnic.[53]

The key to uncovering task resistance is to ask the person why he or she is resisting you in a non-threatening, non-blaming way. The easiest way to get into this mindset is to say, "May I ask why you are resisting this task?" in a curious tone. If you let curiosity drive the conversation, it will come across as a genuine desire instead of resentment. You will then find out what is blocking the person from cooperating with you.

Cal: "May I ask why?"

Intrigued by the concept of uncovering resistance, Cal sat down with his new assistant and said calmly, "I've asked you on several occasions to update the website. I know you're not overworked right now, and this is part of your role here. May I ask why you are putting this off?" She stuttered for a moment, then replied, "To be truthful, I've never updated a website before…it's just a bit outside my comfort zone."

Now, Cal has eased the tension between them, because he has discovered the source of the resistance. By reflecting her behavior back to her and having her acknowledge it, he has put them on the same side of the problem, looking at it together. Now that she has acknowledged her resistance, Cal must work with her to overcome it. The approach he takes will depend on the reason behind the resistance. There are three main reasons a person resists tasks:

1. He is not *competent* in the task yet, so it makes him feel inadequate.

2. The task is *very difficult*, so the person chooses an easier task.
3. The task may expose the person to potential *rejection* from a customer or colleague.

If the person is not competent yet, the solution is to provide coaching for him or her during the initial phases. If the person is avoiding a difficult task, you can offer to "give away" the task to another team member.* This gets the person in touch with his or her desire to conquer the task. If the task involves potential rejection (e.g., sales cold calling), you can work with the person to develop a sales script that brings him the best possible reaction from people. The idea of uncovering resistance may seem obvious. Yet it is not common practice, because most supervisors do not have superior technique in uncovering the resistance. They tend to be passive (ignore the staff member) or aggressive (reprimand him). While there is certainly a time and a place for reprimands, uncovering the resistance comes first.

"I want to be wealthy, not just comfortable."

"Our family makes good money. I want the satisfaction of knowing we are fiscally independent and can pay for vacations and luxuries with cash—as well as have a healthy retirement income," Bill told me with conviction. Bill is a senior executive who commands a high salary in the marketplace. He has always been responsible with money and his family had no consumer debt. Yet, at 47, he is still not close to his dream of financial independence.

Mediocre technique in building wealth

Bill was good at making and saving money, but knew little about the path to true financial freedom. The truth is that Bill had mediocre technique in

*Sometimes, rather than rising to the challenge, there is a chance that the person is relieved that the task has been taken away. At this point, provided you have made many clear requests, have clarified your expectations, and have tried to uncover his resistance, you can consider moving to the reprimand stage. Of course, you must always consult the human resources and legal departments of your organization before proceeding to this stage. For an excellent model of how to handle the reprimand conversation, see Nathaniel Branden's *Self-Esteem At Work: How Confident People Make Powerful Companies*, Jossey-Bass, 1998. For additional training on leadership communication skills, you can also consider The Courage to Win: Mental Toughness for Success 30 Day LIVE Coaching Program. For details, go to http://www.thecouragetowin.com/coachingprogram.html

building wealth. His family had stressed the importance of job security to him and he had focused his efforts on building a secure, rewarding career. This path had served him well—until now. At this stage of his life, Bill was ready to pursue financial wealth, not just security. Bill had never learned a core principle: you must convert earned income into assets that make money for you.

An asset is a vehicle that produces income for you. According to Robert Kyosaki's *What the Rich Invest In That the Poor and Middle Class Do Not*, the three top assets you can build or invest in are:

1. A business
2. Real estate
3. Portfolios (paper investments, such as stocks and bonds)[54]

Managed properly, each of these has the potential to make money for you. The challenge most people have is that they are not financially literate enough to properly choose these vehicles. So, they either lose money or never invest in the first place.

Bill: He started with financial literacy

Bill began by setting a goal to save $50,000 strictly for investment purposes. He knew he couldn't be soft or delusional about the goal, so he used Quicken, a software budgeting program, to ground him each month. Looking at the numbers gave him measurable feedback and recognition for his progress. During this two year period, I gave Bill another assignment: to become financially literate. Bill was careful not to overload himself. First, he learned how to negotiate loans and mortgages at rates far below the average person. Second, he spent six months studying financial statements—creating his own and learning how to evaluate the value of a company using them. Finally, he learned the advantages and disadvantages of stocks, bonds, mutual funds, and real estate.

At the end of two years, Bill had internalized the concept that much successful investing is governed by the principle of buying undervalued vehicles and selling them at a higher price. And, he had enough financial acumen to start getting experience in valuing assets.

Choosing investment vehicles that fit your temperament

At this stage, Bill needed to determine which of the three investment vehicles (a business, stock portfolio or real estate) best fit his temperament. Here are the factors he needed to consider:

Running a business

- You must be able to handle the emotional roller coaster of uncertain cash flow. This means having an alternative source of income in the early phases (or venture capital).
- You must be willing to learn how to sell.
- You must have time to devote to the business.

Stock portfolios

- You must be able to handle the emotional roller coaster of market fluctuations. This means having the patience to invest for the long term.
- You must be willing to learn finance, business, and accounting so you can value companies.
- You must have time to study the markets. Alternatively, you must have a financial broker or investment strategy you trust without reservation—which is rare.

Real estate

- You must be able to handle the emotional roller coaster of making large purchases.
- You must be willing to learn about taxes, borrowing, and negotiating.
- You must have time to travel and value properties.

Bill decided real estate was a good fit for him. Bill enjoyed his career and did not want the stress of running his own business. Plus, his RRSP was already invested in a stock portfolio that was earning him satisfactory returns. Real estate would give him experience in investing and balance his investments at the same time. Starting with his $50,000, Bill bought a property in a popular vacation destination in southern California which had undergone a real estate recession. He arranged for a property manager to rent it out on his behalf, and within one year it had become an asset, bringing him rental income of $300 per month after the mortgage and expenses had been paid. Bill quickly duplicated this success with six new investments in the following five years. By the age of 55, Bill had enough money to choose whether he wanted to keep working or not.

"I'm afraid of choking under pressure."

In 2001, my ringette team was on the verge of a major victory. We were playing our arch-rivals, Edmonton, for the provincial title. I had been cut from the National team the previous summer, causing me to doubt my ability. But I returned the following season anyway. I was nervous. At 34 years old, I was the veteran on the team—a player my teammates might look to for courage. My nerves surprised me a little; they were as strong as I could remember in 28 years of competition. I was having trouble just swallowing normally.

Mediocre technique in handling extreme nerves

Having practiced sport psychology for years, I knew many ways to psyche up for big games. I was well-versed in goal-setting, visualization, pre-game routines, affirmations—all the strategies for creating confidence. But, until this tournament, I had never encountered such extreme nerves—the kind that could render me frozen. I knew I needed superior technique in coping with such anxiety, or I would choke for sure.

"It's OK to be afraid."

Sometimes it's easy to shift our feelings, but other times they have a life of their own. I quickly realized that trying to manipulate my nerves would be futile in this situation. All the traditional techniques—visualizing success, telling myself why I had every reason to be confident—were not working. In fact, they were making me more anxious. Using the principle of self-acceptance, I decided to stop fighting myself. I reasoned that if I could not control my nerves, I should accept them. Of course, the essence of self-acceptance is being open to a feeling with the goal of understanding the request behind the feeling. As far as I could tell, the purpose of nerves was to make me alert and energized to compete—and in a close competition, I would need every ounce of energy possible. Then I remembered that every highly energized, excellent performance of mine was preceded by nerves. Clearly, my nerves would arouse me to a new level of energy—but only if I was open to them. Quietly, I said to myself, "Lisa, it's OK to be afraid." Skating onto the ice, I repeated, "Lisa, it's OK to be afraid." In between whistles, I said to myself, "Lisa, it's OK to be afraid." Every time I said this, I became more relaxed and energized. I scored a goal on the first shift, and the rest is history. My team went on to win the National Championship, and when I was called to receive an all-star award, my coach leaned over and whispered, "No one deserves this more."

I guess it is OK to be afraid.

"My boss won't listen."

Nick's boss was an aggressive leader who questioned Nick's ideas relentlessly. A strong person himself, Nick would fight back when the boss questioned his recommendations. This created an aggressive battle between them, and both men left their conversations feeling dissatisfied and disrespected.

Mediocre technique in resolving conflict

Nick alternated between feeling angry and numb at work. Even though he loved his job, he had fantasies of quitting. Like most people in a conflict, Nick was caught up in the "blame game." He was convinced that his boss could not, and would not, listen.

When a relationship is causing us pain, most of us turn to blame. Blame is a way of denying that we feel helpless to get respect, listening, or affection from another person. Rather than acknowledge our helplessness, we decide that nothing we do will make a difference. This creates lack of trust, and the relationship deteriorates. Because he was caught up in blame, Nick had never realized he had mediocre technique in resolving conflict. I suggested to Nick that he had the power to change these conversations by handling his boss very differently. Fortunately, Nick was objective enough about himself to try something new: the 10% harmony strategy.

The 10% Harmony Strategy

The 10% harmony strategy is a practical, four step process you can use to resolve conflict in any relationship. The purpose of this strategy is simple. Any time a person is upset with you, it is virtually always because he wants something from your relationship—but is not getting it. Your job with the 10% harmony strategy is to discover what the need is and meet it, thereby eliminating the conflict.

Step 1. Fair Enough. Immediately say the phrase, "Fair enough." This suggests that the person you are dealing with is reasonable, which calms him down.

Step 2. Find some truth in at least 10% of what the person is saying. If you agree with him, this diffuses the situation. If you disagree with him, he'll likely become stubborn and escalate the conflict.

Client: "Lisa, this seminar is terrible. Not only did you brush me off this morning when I tried to say hello to you, but I'm not getting anything out of it."

Lisa: "Fair enough. Sometimes at the beginning of a seminar I'm a little preoccupied with getting the equipment set up and I'm not as good a listener as I should be. I'm sorry about that. However, the most important problem seems to be that you feel as though you're wasting your time here."

[Notice that I didn't agree with him that the seminar is terrible. I saw some truth in the fact that I was pre-occupied and showed empathy for his lack of enjoyment in the seminar.]

Step 3. Find out what he wants by asking good questions. Never let anyone criticize you by throwing out sweeping generalizations such as, "You suck, you're an idiot, you're insensitive, you're selfish, you're a jerk. Always ask for clarification. Say, "Exactly how am I a jerk?" so that you can discover what this person wants. [OK, so I am exaggerating a bit here. My point is that you need to ask the person for specifics on his complaint about you.]

Lisa: "May I ask what you were expecting in the seminar?"

Client: "I thought you were going to tell me how to manage my time better...I'm dealing with 236 staff and I'm overwhelmed."

Step 4. Give the person what he wants; or, if you can't, help him try and get it from another source. You can usually find a way to satisfy the request. If not, you can apologize, offer a refund, or ask the person what you can do to help resolve the situation.

Lisa: "Excellent. That's helpful for me to be able to customize this training. Would it be appealing if I included an hour this afternoon on time management?"

Client: "Yes, that would be great."

Nick: Using 10% harmony

For the next three weeks, every time the boss challenged him, Nick would find some truth in at least 10% of what his boss said. "Yes, you're absolutely right—the system we gave the client was not ideal, and certainly this has created headaches for you." After three weeks, Nick realized that his boss only became argumentative when Nick disagreed with him. When Nick disagreed with him, the boss suspected Nick was withholding information, and would attack. Of course, this escalated the conflict.

Instead of arguing, Nick used the 10% harmony strategy and fed the boss information—fast and furious. Before long, Nick was astonished to find the boss accepting his recommendations with few questions—something he never thought would happen.

CHAPTER THIRTEEN

Cultivating the Practice of Competence:

Action Steps

The case studies in this chapter represent only a small number of the challenges you may face in life. Here are two simple action steps you can use to apply the practice of competence to virtually any personal challenge.

1. Determining "what you don't know you don't know."

Write down everything you do not know how to do when it comes to solving your life problem. Here are some categories to consider:

- How to get another person to pursue you for connection or intimacy
- How to get another person to pursue you for ideas or collaboration at work
- How to transition into a new career field (opportunities, jobs, etc.)
- How to manage your time better or be more efficient at work
- How to handle a "bully" at work
- How to excel in sales
- How to surpass revenue goals in your business
- How to delegate your team

To help you with this first exercise, here are some specific examples of completed assignments:

How to excel in sales:

- I don't know a good script for a cold call
- I don't know how to generate a prospect list
- I don't have a good lead generation program that gets customers to call me
- I don't know how to conduct reliable marketing research
- I don't know the psychology behind how people make purchasing decisions
- I don't know how to overcome objections
- I don't know what to say to close a sale

How to get another person to pursue you for connection /intimacy:

- I don't know what makes (person x) turn off and become annoyed
- I don't know what to do when I'm in the presence of (person x) so they find me more attractive, intriguing, etc.
- I don't understand how (person x) makes decisions about our relationship

How to manage your time better and be more efficient at work

- I don't have a system for identifying which tasks are higher priorities than others
- I don't know how to negotiate for extra time on a deliverable
- I don't know how to say "No" to a request in a way that doesn't arouse hostility
- I don't know how to increase my productivity without working more hours

Your list of "what you don't know you don't know":

____

____

____

____

____

____

2. Find help in mentorship, coaching, and education

Whatever problem you are facing, someone on this earth has the solution. It's your responsibility to find this information. In the space below, describe the research you will conduct to find the education and mentors you seek:

Final thoughts

The practice of competence is critical to ensuring that you will gain the superior technique you need to win in your personal challenge.

If you would like some extra help in gaining competence in money, career, sport or relationships—as well as assistance in applying the *Courage to Win* formula to your own life—our team is available to help you.

The Practice of Competence: A Summary

1. After applying self-acceptance and commitment to your life problem, you have clarity and a vision. You are also motivated to act. However, not all actions are created equal. To win, you must take *effective* action.

2. The third and final ingredient in the *Courage to Win* formula is competence. Competence is having superior technique. There are proven success principles in money, relationships, and career. When you internalize them, you develop superior technique. The opposite of competence is mediocre technique.
3. Competence leads to winning for two reasons. First, money, career, and relationships all have a performance element. Second, competence sparks hope in you, which dissolves your last shreds of learned helplessness.
4. The first cornerstone of competence is humility. If you are not winning in relationships, career, or money, someone on this earth has the solution. You must swallow your pride and find it. This means recognizing you 'don't know what you don't know' and finding the right source to help you. The second cornerstone of competence is accountability. Accountability means dropping blame and focusing on your actions.

Here are five proven success principles from our case studies:

1. Triggering attraction. In every relationship, one person is more in touch with the need for connectedness (the pursuer), while the other is more in touch with the need for independence (the pursuee). To keep attraction alive over the long term, you must keep the pursuit dynamic in balance.
2. Removing task resistance. To remove task resistance and gain cooperation from an employee, spouse, friend, or child, you must uncover the reason behind the resistance. You can do this by asking, "May I ask why you are resisting …?"
3. Creating wealth. The rich become wealthy by converting earned income into assets that make them money. There are three main investment vehicles: a business, real estate, and stock portfolios. To invest successfully, you need financial literacy and to select a vehicle that suits your temperament.
4. Calming your nerves under pressure. To calm nerves under pressure, accept them. Use the affirmation, "It's OK to be afraid/nervous/stressed out."

5. Resolving conflict. Whenever you are in conflict with another person, find truth in at least 10% of what he is saying. This will relax him, and you can find out what he needs and resolve the conflict by providing a solution.

Winning: A sacred cause

Thank you for reading. Winning, the ability to move through life challenges, is a sacred cause. When we can manifest our own deepest aspirations, we naturally become more generous and loving towards others. Indeed, love in all its forms is the highest form of winning. I wish you every success in your quest for prosperity, love, and happiness.

Success Tools from The Courage to Win™ Team

The mission of *the Courage to Win™* is to help you realize your highest self by moving you to the next stage of your evolution. For transformational tools to help you win in money, career, love, and sport, go here:

http://www.thecouragetowin.com/tools.html

The Courage to Win™ Coaching Program

Today, you can take control of your destiny by discovering exactly how to apply the formula to your own life through The Courage to Win™: Catapult Yourself to Success 30 Day LIVE Coaching Program with Lisa Lane Brown. The entire focus of this fast-paced LIVE Coaching Program with Lisa is applying the revolutionary *Courage to Win* formula to the key areas of your life that will have the most impact on your career, your relationships, your finances, and your emotional well-being. With this training, you'll know what you really want and how to bring it into reality for yourself—even from the humblest of beginnings. For example, one client was offered TWO senior management positions after just three weeks in this program. Another earned her team a birth to the Olympics. A third client wooed her ex-boyfriend back (he had said there was no hope). Lisa accepts only 10 clients into this program per month. For details, go to: http://www.thecouragetowin.com/coachingprogram.html

FREE 30-day Confidence Building Program

You can collect your FREE 30 Day Confidence Building Program using the *Courage to Win* at http://thecouragetowin.com/confidenceprogram.html

Your success story

We would love to hear your success story using the *Courage to Win* formula. Please send yours to us info@lisabrown.ca. We will respond to every success story.

Endnotes

1. The H.H. the Dalai Lama and Howard C. Cutler, *The Art of Happiness*, Riverhead Books, New York, NY, 1998, p. 16.
2. Brian Tracy, *Something for Nothing*, Thomas Nelson, 2005.
3. Robert Louis Stevenson, *A Christmas Sermon*, Charles Scriber's Sons, New York, NY, 1900.
4. A complete review of this ground-breaking psychological experiment can be found in Martin Seligman, *Learned Optimism: How to Change Your Mind and Your Life*, Vintage Books, New York, NY, 1990, pp. 19-28.
5. Seligman, op. cit. Seligman explains throughout *Learned Optimism* that a core tenant of learned helplessness and pessimism is the conviction that our actions do not matter.
6. Some of these definitions appear in: Phil Laut, *Money is My Friend*, Ballantine Books, New York, 1978, p. 24. Other definitions were inspired by it.
7. Eckhardt Tolle, *The Power of Now*, Namaste Publishing Inc., Vancouver, British Columbia, Canada, 1997.
8. The H.H. the Dalai Lama and Howard C. Cutler, op. cit., pp. 133-134.
9. Tolle, op. cit., p. 31.
10. John Ruskan, *Emotional Clearing*, Broadway Books, New York, NY, 2000, pp. 24-26.
11. Inspired by Nathaniel Branden, *Breaking Free*, Nash Publishing, Los Angeles, CA, 1970. While Branden does not refer to learned helplessness directly, he notes that suppressing feelings also blocks the meaning of the feeling, which makes us impotent to solve the problem we are facing.
12. John Molo, *What I Learned at the Grammys*, Journal of Performance Education, Vol. 1., No. 1., 1996, p. 41.
13. Michael Jordan and Mark Vancil, *For the Love of the Game: My Story*, Crown Publishers Inc., New York, NY, 1998, p. 73.
14. Stu Diver and Simon Bouda, *Survival*, Pan Macmillan, Sydney, Australia, 1999.
15. Seligman, opt. cit. Seligman explains throughout *Learned Optimism* that a core tenant of learned helplessness and pessimism is the conviction that our actions do not matter.
16. John Ruskan, *Emotional Clearing*, Broadway Books, New York, NY, 2000. Ruskan explores the idea that the opposite of suppression is experiencing feelings directly, pp. 160-212.
17. John Ruskan, *Emotional Clearing*, Broadway Books, New York, NY, 2000, p. 24.
18. Sigmund Freud with James Strachey, *The Standard Edition of the Complete Psychological Works of Sigmund Freud*, W.W. Norton & Company, New York, NY, 2000.
19. Phil Laut, *Money is My Friend*, Ballantine Books, New York, NY, 1999, p. 24.
20. Inspired by Branden, *Breaking Free*, opt. cit.
21. Ruskan, opt. cit., p. 24.
22. Janice Berger with Harry Hall, *Emotional Fitness*, Prentice Hall Canada, 2000, p. 166.
23. Ruskan, opt. cit., p. 155.
24. Kevin Trudeau, *Natural Cures "They" Don't Want You to Know About*, Alliance Publishing Group, Elk Grove Village, IL, 2004.
25. Nathaniel Branden, *The Six Pillars of Self-Esteem*, Bantam, New York, NY, 1994, p. 68.
26. Ruskan, opt. cit., p. 23.
27. Branden, *Breaking Free*, opt. cit. Branden discusses in case studies how suppressed painful feelings stemming from childhood trauma morphs into self-limiting conclusions and beliefs.
28. Ruskan, opt. cit., p. 279.
29. Sentence completion techniques were pioneered by Nathaniel Branden. He presents an explanation of them in *The Six Pillars of Self-Esteem*, Bantam, New York, NY, 1994, p. 82 and p. 308.

30. Donna Eden, *Energy Medicine*, Jeremy P. Tarcher/Putnam, New York, NY, 1998, p. 133.
31. Eden, opt cit. For an in-depth review of the body's energy chakras, see pp. 133-171.
32. Inspired by Laut, opt. cit., p. 24.
33. Ruskan, opt. cit., p. 136.
34. Celine Dion, *My Story, My Dream*, Avon Books, 2000, pp. 227-240.
35. Nathaniel Branden, *The Six Pillars of Self-Esteem*, Bantam, New York, NY, 1994, pp. 118-123.
36. Carole Talbot-Honeck and Terry Orlick, *The Essence of Excellence: Mental Skills of Top Classical Musicians*, Journal of Excellence, Issue No. 1, 1998, p. 63.
37. Rhonda Bryne, *The Secret*, Atria Books, New York, NY, 2006, p. 7-8.
38. Dr. Wayne Dyer and Dr. Deepak Chopra, *How to Get What You Really, Really, Really, Really Want (Audio Cassette)*, Hay House, Inc. 1998.
39. Mark Tewksbury, Speech, *Visions of Excellence*, Calgary, Alberta, Canada, 2000.
40. Eckhardt Tolle, *The Power of Now*, Hodder & Stoughton, 2005.
41. Donald J. Trump, *The Art of the Deal*, Warner Books, New York, NY, 1989, p. 46.
42. Mark Tewksbury, *Visions of Excellence*, Penguin, Toronto, Ontario, Canada, 1993.
43. Seligman, opt. cit. I describe only one dimension of optimism, which is the ability to explain negative life events in a temporary way. Seligman presents two other dimensions (pervasiveness and personalization) on pp. 46-52.
44. Seligman, opt. cit., pp. 223-228. I present a simplified version of Seligman's cognitive approach to invoking optimism.
45. Jerry Seinfeld, *Sein Language*, Bantam Books, New York, NY, 1993, p. 3.
46. Audrius Barzdukas, *Standing First in Line*, Journal of Performance Education, Vol. 1, No. 1, 1996, p. 24.
47. Tom Hanson, *The Mental Aspects of Hitting in Baseball: A Case Study of Hank Aaron*, Journal of Performance Education, Vol. 1, No. 1, 1996, p. 63.
48. Donald Trump, *The Art of the Deal*, Warner Books, New York, NY, 1989, pp. 65-80.
49. Homer MacDonald, *Stop Your Divorce* and www.stopyourdivorce.com, 1998.
50. Stuart Wilde, *Silent Power*, Hay House, Inc., USA, 1996, p. 19.
51. Wilde, op. cit., pp. 19-20.
52. Inspired by ideas presented in Homer MacDonald's *Stop Your Divorce*, www.stopyourdivorce.com, 1998.
53. Dr. Terry Orlick, *Nice On My Feelings*, Creative Bound Inc., Carp Ontario, 1995, p. 40-41.
54. Robert T. Kiyosaki with Sharon L. Lechter, *Rich Dad's Guide to Investing*, Warner Business Books, 2000, New York, NY, pp. 120-124.

ABOUT THE AUTHOR

Lisa Lane Brown is a professional speaker, author and coach who helps people win using mental toughness. A former world class athlete, Lisa is the author of the Courage to Win formula, which she has taught to thousands of achievers worldwide. Visit the Courage to Win site at www.thecouragetowin.com.

Author photographed by Shannon Hutchison